SCHOOL PHILANTHROPY
HANDBOOK

PRAISE FOR THE *SCHOOL PHILANTHROPY HANDBOOK*

It is rare to be able to access the deep expertise and wise counsel of a genuinely expert practitioner in such a concise and well-structured book. So many great messages and much values-based guidance. Definitely a must read.

Emeritus Professor Glenn Bowes AO
MBBS PhD FRACP
Former Associate Dean Advancement,
University of Melbourne

A combination of vision, values, strategy, compelling communication via stories and practical advice make this a significant resource for school leaders. Philanthropy is not fundraising. If you are unsure of the difference, this is the book for you.

Allan Shaw
Ass Dip Art Grad Dip Ed MEd UTAS FACEL FACE
Former CEO AHISA
Past principal of The Knox School and
Peter Moyes Anglican Community School

There are a number of things common across third sector organisations; one is the need for friend and fundraising, another is how inexperienced the sector is in achieving either. This book provides an accessible, 'hands on' guide, written by an expert in the field with supportive tools to start or refine your approach to attract and retain philanthropic support. Whilst the book has a school focus, the contents extend to all third sector organisations.

Dr John Ballard
BA MHA DBA GAICD
Company director
Former Associate Vice Chancellor ACU and NFP CEO

The accumulated wisdom and experience in this book are invaluable. It is a resource every independent school needs.

Gabby Montagnese
ABPB MAICD
Former CEO New Age Caravans
Active philanthropist
Board member, Eltham College

I admire anyone who has the courage to write about culture. And I particularly admire someone who encourages a culture of giving to support something as essential as education.

This book should be compulsory reading for anyone contemplating a school fundraising program. It contains the wisdom of a lifetime's devotion to this critical task.

Simon McKeon AO
BCom LLB Melb. HonDPH La Trobe FAICD
Chancellor, Monash University
2011 Australian of the Year

SCHOOL PHILANTHROPY
HANDBOOK

How to build a culture of giving

Gavan Woinarski

amba press

Copyright © Gavan Woinarski 2023

All rights reserved. No part of this book may be reproduced or transmitted in any form or by any means, electronic or mechanical, including photocopying, recording or by any information storage and retrieval system, without prior permission in writing from the publisher.

Published by Amba Press
Melbourne, Australia
www.ambapress.com.au

Editor – Beth Browne
Cover Designer – Tess McCabe

ISBN: 9781922607461 (pbk)
ISBN: 9781922607478 (ebk)

A catalogue record for this book is available from the National Library of Australia.

CONTENTS

About the Author		ix
Acknowledgements		xi
Chapter 1	Introducing Philanthropy	1
Chapter 2	A Culture of Philanthropy	11
Chapter 3	Philanthropy in Schools	25
Chapter 4	Fundraising in Schools	53
Chapter 5	Community Relations	59
Chapter 6	The Future of Philanthropy in Schools	69
Appendices		77
Appendix 1	Key Elements of a Culture of Philanthropy in a School	78
Appendix 2	Philanthropy Working Party Terms of Reference	80
Appendix 3	Philanthropy Working Party Meeting Guidelines	82
Appendix 4	Memorandum of Gift Template	84
Appendix 5	Memorandum of Understanding Template	89
Appendix 6	Functions Checklist	91
Appendix 7	Gift Submission Example: Student Leadership Program	94
Appendix 8	Donation/Pledge Form Template	96

Appendix 9	Receipt Letter Example	98
Appendix 10	Bequest Form Template	99
Appendix 11	Codicil Template	101
Appendix 12	Thanking Guidelines	103
Appendix 13	Donor Commitment Continuum	105
Appendix 14	Useful Words and Phrases	106
Glossary		109
Bibliography		113

ABOUT THE AUTHOR

Gavan Woinarski is the Principal Consultant at GDZW Philanthropy at its Best. Gavan began his career in philanthropy and fundraising in 1995 after a distinguished career as a teacher and educational leader in Australia and the United Kingdom. After 11 years in educational fundraising at Melbourne Grammar School and Methodist Ladies' College he moved to the health sector as Director of the Mercy Health Foundation. Here he established several endowed Chairs and built a corpus of $15m in 8 years.

Gavan consults to families and individuals encouraging them to realise the potency of endowments and to make gifts that can empower people. When working with schools and organisations' senior leadership and board members he stresses the importance of establishing an enduring culture of philanthropy for the school; this will outlast short-term fundraising activities.

Gavan willingly shares his accumulated wisdom and experience with schools large and small, in cities and rural centres.

ACKNOWLEDGEMENTS

Investing time and energy into writing a book was a new experience for me. My naivete was soon realised when I discovered how much time and effort it takes to collect all the ideas and information that I needed to share. Then there was choosing the words in the right order and sequence to make the meaning clear. This has been an enjoyable undertaking and professionally rewarding, because it enabled me to assess and clarify my thoughts and concepts.

There are many people I wish to thank and acknowledge who, in various ways, have contributed to this book.

Alicia Cohen from Amba Press who had faith in me from the start. Beth Browne for her editorial skills that polished the text and Liz Duff for proof reading large extracts of my manuscript.

I want to thank Simon Le Plastrier because he encouraged me to write the *Philanthropy Reference Manual* that morphed to become this book.

The friends at my croquet club deserve some recognition. They slowly came to 'get it' and understand me and listened to my stories.

Henry Birman, of Studio HBD, for creating inspiring visuals to compliment my ideas and thoughts.

Ann Badger is important because she gave me my first job in my career change from teacher to the realm of philanthropy.

Former Principal and CEO, Allan Shaw, engaged me to build an enduring culture of philanthropy at The Knox School. His grasp of community relations, his patience and common sense are admirable, as is his saying "Do it once, do it right."

Dr John Ballard who saw my bewilderment when I started to build the Mercy Health Foundation. Once he took a sheet of paper from the printer and handed it to me indicating I had a blank canvas, start where you like and go for it.

Geoff and Helen Handbury deserve a special mention. Their approach to philanthropy emphasised the importance of giving for the betterment of people.

I have especially enjoyed working with and learning from James Angus, Glenn Bowes, Colin Carter, Glyn Davis, Mike Fitzpatrick, Tom Kudelka, Cliff and Jane Gale, Andrew Grimwade, Will Hamilton, Beth Higgs, John Higgins, Sue Karzis, John Lewis, John Matthies, Linda Mellors, Barry O'Callaghan, Philip Mayers, John McLeod, Barry McIlwaine, Gabby Montagnese, Maria Myers, Nigel Peck, Rob Phillpot, Steve Rothfield, Paul Sheahan, David Smorgon, Paul Wheelton, Sue Walker and the BBT team at Morgan Stanley.

I am also most grateful for the eye-opening experience of working with Yorta Yorta people Paul Briggs and his niece and Kylie.

I have come to know many people over the years that have become donors and friends. It was the engagement with these people and connecting them with their interests that was the best part of the experience. I simply thank and acknowledge all those people who are a part of this book. They will know who they are.

CHAPTER 1

INTRODUCING PHILANTHROPY

I first came into contact with philanthropy on a warm autumn afternoon when I visited a couple in their home. They had recently moved from their farm into the regional town of Deniliquin. I had met these people about eight months earlier at a reunion for past boarders of the school I was working in as Development Manager. I remember introducing myself at the reunion during a gap in the proceedings that allowed for informal mingling. They were clearly enjoying the occasion and knew lots of people at the function. Family members were included in the invitation, so I began our conversation by asking about their family and ties to the district.

I discovered they were both from the area and the children of farmers. They had been on their farm for 52 years before selling up and retiring to live in the local town. They met at a dance in the town's mechanics hall and were married in the local church six months later. Their honeymoon was a road trip in an FJ Holden to Sydney, 600 kilometres eastwards, where they wanted to swim in the ocean and see the Harbour Bridge.

They certainly were part of the local community, being involved in the Country Women's Association, Rotary and the local farmers' network. I listened to stories of floods, droughts and some mighty dust storms. I learned about the rise and fall of their fortunes as the prices of wool, crops and livestock rose and fell. They joked that when the wool price rose, they had few sheep to sell because the drought had caused them to reduce the size of their flock. When the prices recovered, their flock was only just large enough to keep them going. They were cheerful about the vagaries of farming.

When I arrived at their house months later, I was struck by its modesty. The purpose of my visit was to collect an envelope. Previously, we had enjoyed phone conversations about supporting a student to attend the school as a boarder, preferably someone from their district. Over tea and chocolate cake on the back veranda, I learned they each had one sibling but no children. They had a strong desire that children from rural areas should enjoy good educational prospects. The husband handed me an envelope as I was leaving. The couple thanked me for coming and wished me a safe journey for the four-hour drive back home.

I was itching to open the envelope and presumed it contained a cheque. On the outskirts of the town, I stopped to open the envelope. There were two items inside. One was a thank-you letter written by the husband to the current headmaster explaining how much he had enjoyed being at the school. He shared some stories about a few teachers and the arduous all-day journey between school and home at the start and end of each term. There was a cheque inside the envelope, and the sum was equivalent to a year's tuition and boarding fees. Here was a modest couple supporting someone they did not know. It showed they had faith in the school and demonstrated their belief in education. I wondered if they should be described as philanthropists.

WHAT IS PHILANTHROPY?

Philanthropy is defined as 'the love of humankind'. It involves the giving of time, information, goods, services or money to improve the wellbeing of other people and the community. Its Greek origin comes from two words: *philos*, meaning friend, and *anthropos*, meaning people. Essentially, philanthropy improves the lives of people.

Philanthropy's early roots can be traced back to the stories, legends and treatises of ancient cultures in South America, Europe, the Middle East and Asia. Circa 1800 BP, the Egyptian Book of the Dead made it clear that passage to the afterlife depended on a life full of benevolent acts. The ancient Egyptians believed their deities expected those seeking immortality to have done good during their life. Similarly, the Qur'an describes the sharing of wealth with the less fortunate as an obligation. It expresses the importance of bringing a benefit and blessing to the world.

Alms for the poor have been given by the British sovereign for centuries. Each year on Maundy Thursday the sovereign attends a service in a cathedral and invites those in need to join. For several centuries specially minted one penny, two pence, three pence and four pence coins were given to the poor at the end of the service. Numismatics seek these coins as rare and highly desirable collectable items. In modern times these obsolete denominations have been replaced by gifts of the current currency presented in a purse. This annual act of kindness is an example of the love of humankind.

In 1622 an American Indigenous leader known as Squanto taught the newly arrived Pilgrims how to grow corn and where to fish. His kindness meant the Pilgrims survived their first year following a harsh winter and dwindling supplies.

Education has often been the impetus for philanthropy, where the foresight of donors can be enjoyed by future generations of students, staff and academics. John Harvard left his library and estate to found a university. Elihu Yale's gift established a college in 1701 that later evolved to become a university. In 1885 Leland and Jane Stanford donated a sum to found Stanford University.

Philanthropy has led to some unusual and unique stories. One centres on James Smithson, an Englishman who died in 1829 and left his estate for the benefit of others to found the Smithsonian Institution in Washington, DC. He had a lifelong interest in science and published several papers by the Royal Society on topics such as chemistry and mineralogy. He had never visited the United Sates but wanted to invest in this new country.

Another unusual philanthropic instance occurred when a school inherited a sum of money, the income from which was to pay for the school fees for the sons of Boer War veterans. This gift was important at the time because it provided opportunities for these students. But as the years went past, it became clear that the bequest could not continue to be honoured. While this gift caused some curious legal challenges 40 years later, it provided an example for others in the school community to consider. It became a building block of an enduring culture of philanthropy at the school.

PHILANTHROPY IN AUSTRALIA

In Australia there is evidence of philanthropy all around us, where gifts have been made for the benefit of humanity. One example is the Felton Bequest. Alfred Felton and his business partner, Frederick Grimwade, ran a successful wholesale druggist company. Felton died in 1904 and left the bulk of his estate to establish the Felton bequest. Most of the income from this perpetual trust goes to the National Gallery of Victoria to support art acquisitions, and a smaller portion supports general charitable purposes. Since it began, the Felton bequest has bought artworks that are now collectively valued at more than $2 billion.

Sir Macpherson Robertson made his fortune from confectionary manufacturing. Some of his well-known brands are Freddo Frogs, Crunchie and Cherry Ripe. His interest in supporting women's education was evident when, in 1934, he donated the necessary sum to build a secondary school in Melbourne dedicated to girls' education. The school is now affectionately known as Mac.Rob High.

The Wyatt Trust was established with a bequest from Dr William Wyatt in 1886. It is a perpetual trust that distributes its annual income to assist South Australians who are in need. Dr Wyatt was held in such high regard that the trust was established by an act of parliament.

The Gordon Darling Foundation was established in 1991 to support visual arts activities throughout Australia and was established by a bequest. We can only speculate that Gordon was motivated to establish a perpetual trust in his name because of examples provided by others.

In 1954 the Carnegie Corporation of New York and the Rockefeller Foundation combined to make a gift to fund the building of a radio telescope near the town of Parkes in New South Wales. This telescope positioned Australia as a leader within the global astronomical community. It was used to relay messages to NASA during moon landings, so it was pivotal in the landing of a man on the moon. Two overseas grant makers saw an opportunity to support a visionary project in a country that was unfamiliar with major philanthropic contributions, and their gift had a much larger impact than was first expected.

In 2001 three families combined to donate $150 to start the Tasmanian Land Conservancy. They then went on to secure funding from a variety of sources and recruited community groups and volunteers to support the conservancy's vision for Tasmania to become a global leader in nature conservation. Tasmanians now hold their natural assets in high regard. The biosecurity protections currently in place at air and sea ports in Tasmania can be traced back to the first meeting of the Tasmanian Land Conservancy. Collective endeavour and the power of the voice can make a huge difference.

THE EVOLUTION OF PHILANTHROPY

For a long time, philanthropy and making donations was a quiet and understated activity that attracted little attention. Donors preferred anonymity, and making donations was a private matter. The size of their donations was kept hidden, and seeking recognition was shunned. But times have changed. Donors, families, businesses, trusts and foundations now want to champion how their donations make a difference. Some billionaires have pledged to give away substantial portions of their fortunes in their lifetime. They want to see and feel the benefit of their donations and provide an example for others to follow. Many believe giving should be a proud tradition.

Philanthropy is becoming more familiar because more stories about philanthropy are being shared on various media platforms. We are hearing stories about Australians, as well as people from other countries, who have promised to donate large sums of money during their lifetime to causes they like and admire, and they are often described as philanthropists. When people are described as philanthropic, it says more about their character and values than their wealth. This is because philanthropy is not about money—money is really the vehicle—it is about giving to help others or to improve a community's prospects and prosperity.

Philanthropy is not confined to bold actions or large sums. Modest acts of kindness and generosity can also be described as philanthropic. In the school context, there is often an informal group that keeps an eye on others and regularly lends a hand when needed. Such seemingly small acts add up to something much bigger—the values present in the school's culture—and they shine a light on the goodness of helping those in need and being philanthropic.

Apart from individuals and families who make annual donations, there are trusts and foundations that make grants each year to their chosen areas of interest. Some of these entities are relatively well known—for example, the Myer Foundation, the Wyatt Trust and the Vincent Fairfax Family Foundation. Then there are trust companies, such as Perpetual and Equity Trustees, which manage funds that were donated or bequeathed for specific purposes.

Many corporations—large and small, public and private—have established a granting program, often via a vehicle they call a foundation. These programs demonstrate to their stakeholders and clients that they are good corporate citizens and allow them to support charities that align with their core business interests. For example, the Marshall White real estate agency has established a foundation to support homeless people, and some mining companies support local communities near their mines with grants or give to the Royal Flying Doctor Service to buy aircraft to deliver medical care to remote communities.

There are about 54,000 organisations registered with the Australian Charities and Not-for-profits Commission (ACNC). They range from small kindergarten parents' groups seeking donations for playground equipment, which report gifts of some thousands of dollars, to national organisations, such as Teach for Australia, which report donations of more than a million dollars each year. As a result of this activity, philanthropy has been elevated in people's consciousness.

THE PHILANTHROPIC VOICE

Philanthropy's best advocate is the voice. To illustrate this notion, we can look at the work of Rosie Batty. Her stance to eliminate domestic violence illustrates the power of a person's voice to promote change and improve the lives of others. The changes Rosie advocates involve leadership from politicians, government departments, service providers and agencies. Money is not the main ingredient to facilitate this change; over time a culture will evolve that abhors domestic violence. Rosie's voice has made a difference, and she has been philanthropic because of her love for humankind.

Independent schools have access to many voices. Most older independent schools have an established development office (or similar) that concentrates on building relationships with past staff, current parents and alumni, the three groups that are a school's main philanthropic stakeholders. These groups are the most likely to make a gift when the time is right. Over the years, these older schools have received many donations, some quite large, especially as bequests. They boast impressive facilities and have stories about how gifts were secured and the pride the donors had in making their donation. Have these schools built a culture of philanthropy, or have they simply been in close contact with wealthy families?

Major capital campaigns involve getting many large gifts before the formal announcement of the campaign is shared with the community. In the end, the campaign is completed, money has been raised and a celebratory event hosted. The challenge is to look at the statistics. Let's say the school's database of all its constituents comprises 12,000 people. If 435 people donated to the campaign, does this reveal a culture of philanthropy? What if 1,756 gave? Would this give a different picture?

These capital campaigns have incentivised newer independent schools to copy the older schools' model, with mixed success. A newer independent school with a philanthropic mindset will set aside a budget to invest in building relationships with its community. Two or three donors might be inspired to cover half the costs of a scholarship for two years. It is important to concentrate on the future and on building relationships rather than the receipt book.

Running a development office and building relationships takes time and costs money. Newer independent schools often put their toe in the water and set up a fundraising position without having in place all the necessary back-end elements of a development office. After some time, the office becomes difficult to justify because the income from donations does not cover all the costs of events and staff time. Eventually, the development office or fundraising position is scaled back and an opportunity is lost.

We need to appreciate it takes two years to establish meaningful connections within the school hierarchy and with all the school's constituents. People will donate and become regular supporters if a school takes the time to focus on meaningful relations rather than donations. For example, establishing a bequest society—something that is appealing to alumni and past staff—takes two years to get going. But once it is established, it is an enduring and strategic investment in a school's philanthropic future. Generally, a development office begins to pay for itself after three years, and after five years, the school will be well ahead. Without a functioning development office, community relations programs and community engagement will effectively stagnate. The parents' association and alumni group will probably continue, with the two groups operating separately.

Many schools have wonderful stories of donors making large donations in support of a particular project, such as a new classroom block, science facility or sportsground. These people are often described as being philanthropic. Is this the case, or are they simply being generous? A family that gives a six-figure gift can make an enormous difference to a school, and they should be thanked and acknowledged. But we may not know if the gift was easily managed by the donor. Was it in fact generous? Was it philanthropic? Was it to seek attention? These questions prompt us to think in a different way. If the donor of a large sum can use their voice to advocate the cause, their gift will inspire others, the results will multiply and a culture of giving will be underway.

And then of course there is language. Should a school have 'targets' or 'prospective donors'? Will the committee 'hit them up' or 'connect and inspire them'? Does a school want to 'get donations' or 'secure gifts'? The language we use can be very influential for donors and determine how a culture of philanthropy is implanted in a school community's psyche. Strong cultures outlast fashion and vogue. The ultimate outcome of a philanthropic culture is that people are inspired to make a gift they are proud of, and the size of their gift is less important. Further information about the language of philanthropy and best-practice communication are included in Appendix 14.

The following chapters explore the notion of philanthropy in independent schools, including how it can advance a school's capacity to provide exceptional education and improve educational outcomes for students. School leaders will gain the tools and knowledge to establish an enduring culture of philanthropy in their school. From hints and tips to templates and guidelines, with some amazing stories shared along the way, this book provides a refreshed look at how schools can embrace philanthropy in a contemporary context.

CHAPTER 2

A CULTURE OF PHILANTHROPY

The culture of a school is an important and powerful asset. You cannot touch it, but you can feel it. When people come into contact with a school, they will feel its culture straightaway. A school's culture is a combination of many ingredients, including its history, location, uniform, gender mix and religious affiliation, to name a few. The culture is the main influencer when people interact with your school. What do you want people to remember after they come to your school?

THE IMPORTANCE OF CULTURE

The memories of my first few days at school helped me understand the importance of culture. I wanted to go to school, and I was excited about the first day. I thought my school days would be filled with stories and games and that I would learn to count, read and play on the oval. The local primary school I attended was different to what I expected. The teachers were strict, and the Grade 6 boys were rough and ruled the playground.

Students were warned to follow the rules and not be a nuisance. No-one knew my name. One day in the first few weeks of my first term, I was accidently knocked, and my precious vegemite sandwich fell onto the ground. I brushed off the dirt and began to eat. Others around me yelped in surprise. Soon I was attracting unwanted attention and the teasing began. I became the dirt boy. I sought help from my class teacher and was ignored. I then asked one of the senior boys to be my friend, but this did not work. I withdrew from the hustle of school life, sat in the back row, became reserved and wondered why schools were important. *What's good about this place?* I asked myself. The next year, I changed schools and my life improved. At my new school the teachers knew my name and they smiled. I got to use my pencil, learned to count and read, and the playground was always fun. I can still remember the unsmiling culture of my first school.

A school's culture encompasses thinking, behaviours, decisions and actions and influences how it treats and manages its students, staff, parents and other key constituents. In return, those in contact with the school behave in response to how they are treated and respected; it is a two-way street.

Over the years, I have visited many schools. Many were in London when I was teaching in a preparatory school and studying at university. Others were in California after a Council for Advancement and Support of Education conference or in Boston during an educational study trip. In every instance I can recall accurately how I felt as a visitor at that school. The names of those I met have faded, but the feeling remains.

When we travel, we experience different cultures. In preparation for our visit to other countries, we might draw up a list of sights to visit. Some will be man-made and others natural wonders. Visiting a sight of natural beauty or an ancient monument creates unforgettable pictures and memories to share on our return home. But it is the act of travelling to those places and the people we meet that add so much more to our experience. We hear different languages and unfamiliar musical instruments, eat different foods, see different styles of dress, learn about other religions and travel on conveyances that challenge our sense of survival. It is the cultures we encounter that so often make the biggest impression.

The name of an organisation, its logo, its tagline and the livery it uses are very visible assets. Combined, these elements create a recognisable brand and convey a message, and over time they become familiar. As a result, we know instantly what these organisations do, sell or create. When we think of Apple and its apple logo, it immediately makes a connection. Because of its reputation, range of products and almost ubiquitous use, we quickly and easily relate to what the logo and name mean. Other comparable global brands include the purple colour and cursive script of Cadbury, for instance, and the blue oval badge of the Ford Motor Company. Similarly, it is alleged that Coca-Cola is the only brand name and script that is recognised in every country on earth and the words 'Coca-Cola' can be understood in any language. These are the obvious external assets of an organisation, but there are internal assets that are equally or more important.

Connected to brands is a certain feeling. When we think of Qantas, we think of the kangaroo on the tail of its aircraft and its advertisements featuring the song *I Still Call Australia Home*, which create a feeling of warmth or nostalgia. The name Rolls-Royce conveys a different feeling; it is associated with wealth, status and engineering excellence, and there is little emotion. An organisation's structure, location, industry and size influence how it functions. These characteristics determine its efficiency and therefore its success. But there is something else present that is less obvious, even tacit, which can be felt but not seen. It is culture.

RESPONSIBILITY FOR CULTURE

Responsibility for culture starts with an organisation's leadership. The school board or council is responsible for three important aspects of a school's operations:

1. strategy
2. appointment of the principal
3. culture.

All of the board's duties and responsibilities emanate from these three core functions.

In every business there are a multitude of areas that need supervision and careful management, including finance, governance, risk, facilities, staff wellbeing, legal obligations, logistics and service delivery, to name but a few. Trained specialist staff are employed to cover these areas, and their combined endeavour makes the business run smoothly. However, the strategic direction—the priority given to what is to be supervised and managed—starts with the board.

For a school, there are additional areas to address, such as the quality of student learning, the school's reputation, enrolments, staffing, student and staff wellbeing, staff professional development, parents and community engagement. All of these areas need trained and highly skilled professionals to make the school operate effectively. When staff concentrate solely on their area of expertise, without insights into the whole organisation or alignment with its culture, then there is a risk of discordance that could threaten efficiency and reputation.

Underpinning everything a school does is its culture. A school's culture reflects its values, how it cares for and respects people and prioritises its resources. To illustrate this point, the following case study is a hypothetical example of a good school culture at work.

Case Study 1
School Culture in Action

The parents of a year 11 student, an only child, were killed in a plane crash. It took some time for the child's parents' estate and financial matters to be settled, yet his school fees needed to be paid. And what of the student's welfare? The school quickly agreed to waive the fees for a while and swiftly motivated its staff to offer the student appropriate support. Next, members of the school community offered help, such as friendship, accommodation and legal advice.

In times of crisis or need, a school's culture quickly comes to the surface. As COVID-19 expanded its impact, home-based learning became the norm. Households adjusted their routines, and the kitchen table soon became an office or classroom for many. Electronic communication became ever-present and interpersonal connections via videoconferencing and email increased. In one case, a parent realised that some students in the school may not have had a computer at home. Further investigation revealed some families had only one computer to be shared amongst two or more children. The school community wanted to help. A plea to the community raised enough money to purchase computers so that children in four families could participate in home-based learning. The question answered was: *How can I use what I have to help others?*

Establishing a culture of philanthropy, the love of humankind, is a unique undertaking for any independent school. Once established, this love of humankind should sit within the school's culture. Such a culture will provide an enduring legacy and lasting benefits, which will be evidenced by the depth of the school's community engagement and an array of favourable comments heard amongst its constituents. As a result, informal peer-to-peer comments will reflect well on the school. From this goodwill, the school will collect more friends, more advocates, more donors and more donations. The donations may be in the form of time volunteered, word-of-mouth endorsements (advocacy), gifts-in-kind or money. This is a philanthropic culture at work, and the lasting outcome will be the collection of friends.

Culture can be regarded as touchy-feely, and because it cannot be easily seen or measured it usually fails to garner the support it deserves. However, culture is a critical success factor and reveals a great deal about a school: its values, its priorities and what makes it tick. It is about *how we do things around here*. A positive culture can also withstand the complexities of a crisis or traumatic event because when people feel connected they will pull together.

A school's culture emanates from its founders. Why did they start the school? A school's leaders should bear the founders' intentions and vision in mind in the current context. I mentioned this at a meeting with a board member of a school I know quite well. I learned a few weeks later that the board member phoned a member of the founding board to find out the motivation for starting the school. During a subsequent meeting they looked though some old files and found the minutes of the first board meeting. The exact minute that mentioned the founding of a school was discovered and the words were copied and placed on the landing page of the school's website. A historical element of the school's evolution was shared for others to enjoy.

Table 1 below outlines how parents might value a school and what that school believes. The elements listed relate to culture and create a mutual pathway for engagement.

Table 1: Cultural Elements Associated with a School

Parents	School
Value education	Provides educational excellence and strives for a personal best for each student
Seek connection and being part of a community	Welcomes and includes its community
Admire teachers and teaching	Has staff with high educational standards and a passion for their craft
Have pride in their children's school	Seeks to be a sectoral leader, provides leadership and exhibits positively *how we do things around here*
Want value for their money	Is financially sound and well managed

This table can be extended and varied to reflect the different stakeholders of a school. We could substitute parents for students or donors, for example. The important point is to consider how a school can meet the expectations of its constituents.

Principals and board members may understand that a culture of philanthropy is important, but they may be uncertain about where to start and what resources are required to establish and sustain the culture. Sometimes a committee is formed to examine how this could be achieved. The committee might organise a series of focus groups seeking input and comment from the school's constituents or conduct an online survey. Some schools might host an open forum. Those invited to participate are often known to the school because this reduces the risk of adverse comments or findings. However, engaging only with existing friends will limit the breadth of input the school receives when there is a need to learn from as diverse a range of stakeholders as possible. There is generally an enthusiastic initial response, but people become sceptical when the word 'philanthropy' is used because they think it is all about asking people to donate money. It is not; it is about connecting and inspiring people so they know that philanthropy concentrates on improving the lives of others and the communities in which we live and work.

When a school defines where it wants to go and how it wants to behave, a clearer and bigger picture emerges. Faith-based schools may draw on their faith for guidance, while non-denominational schools will substantiate their behaviours by their values. Whatever the case, a clearly defined board strategy shared with a school's constituents and acted on by senior staff gives direction and confidence to everyone.

Many schools list their values on their mastheads, letterhead and website with a tagline that summarises their point of difference. Table 2 overleaf provides an example of how a school might elucidate and transmit its principles and values to its community. By clarifying its principles, a school makes the importance of its beliefs and values coherent and easily understood, with greater meaning than a single tagline.

Table 2: School Principles and Corresponding Behaviours

Our principles	Our behaviours
We are ambitious	We resource our students and staff
We are innovators	We evaluate ideas, old and new
We are sustainable	We are financially sound and environmentally astute
Everyone is respected	We nurture every student's talent
Students are our main focus	We organise ourselves so students come first
Opportunities are offered without bias	We avoid stereotypes and ingrained assumptions
Our faith is our guide	We promote inclusion and tolerance

Such a simple table can be placed on the school's website or in its handbook. When used in enrolment documentation, it can give confidence to future parents that they are considering a school that has a caring and vibrant culture.

In many cases, a lack of knowledge and experience, no clear plan and a misunderstanding about philanthropy results in this noble idea drifting into the too-hard basket. Interest wanes and an opportunity is lost. To prevent this from happening we should focus on the true meaning of philanthropy. When this is shared with the community, the scepticism and misconception that philanthropy equals money evaporates. When the topic of philanthropy arises, the first questions to address should be:

- *What needs improving?*
- *What needs supporting?*
- *How can I use what I have been given to benefit others?*

None of these questions are about money. The school board should therefore consider how it might begin establishing a culture of philanthropy by looking at its messaging and marketing.

The composition of a school board should include people who represent the different constituents of its community and provide a cross-section of opinion and different perspectives. The board often has subgroups such as audit and finance, building and grounds, risk and governance, communications and marketing, and strategic planning. What is frequently absent is a subgroup charged with culture and community, yet this is so important.

BUILDING A PHILANTHROPIC CULTURE: A NEW MODEL

Establishing a resilient culture of philanthropy in a school requires a board decision followed by a commitment ensuring the necessary investment of resources, time and money will be made. The depth and enduring success of such a culture will depend on:

- the commitment of the school's leaders
- the school's consistent and careful messaging about the true meaning of philanthropy
- recruiting active advocates (people who speak well of the school, its teachers and its results)
- how the school cares for students and staff
- how the school values its community.

It should take about three to five years to establish a lasting philanthropic culture in a school. Change is apparent after 12 to 15 months, and momentum starts to build after 18 months. The most important element of such a culture is active advocates, those who will lend their voice. These people will exemplify the potency of peer-to-peer connections and are critical to capturing the hearts and minds of your key stakeholders.

> **Case Study 2**
> **The Potency of Peer-to-Peer Connections**
>
> Two parents with three children at a school wanted to make a gift to endow an award for one of the school's values—in this case, respect. Such an award required $5,000 to be endowed, but the parents could only give half that amount. In a casual conversation in the school car park another parent became interested in this idea. So two sets of parents combined their resources to endow the gift, showing the potency of collective endeavour and the value of peer-to-peer connections.

Independent schools often have a parents' association, an alumni association and sometimes a foundation. These three subgroups require specific, individual reporting and, depending on their legal structure, three sets of audited accounts to supervise and maintain. They will also entail discrete political settings for the principal to manage, and they usually operate apart from one another. They are siloed. Merging these three groups into one is worth considering.

There are many benefits of having one unified body that represents the main constituents of a school. This group should have representatives from parents, alumni, staff, past staff and friends—for example, grandparents and local community leaders. Past staff can give a perspective on the evolution of the school and often correct popular misconceptions that may have become accepted fact. Alumni have insights into the resources a school needs to maintain healthy alumni relations, such as the database, archives and the logistics of hosting a reunion on school grounds. Parents can gain an insight into the complexity of running a school and the interrelations between each constituent group. With collective knowledge, a deeper understanding of philanthropy emerges and healthy discussions can take place about how donations could be secured and how donors should be thanked and stewarded. Such a group could be called the Philanthropy Working Party (PWP).

The members of each constituency should see themselves as the current custodians of their school. Their different responsibilities and roles are summarised below.

Table 3: School Constituencies and Their Responsibilities

School Constituencies	Responsibilities
School Board	The school board provides the necessary leadership and resources to support the philanthropic culture of the school. Board members: • are advocates and donors • support the resourcing necessary to build and maintain a culture of philanthropy • ensure the board agenda includes Philanthropy Working Party (PWP) reports • attend functions when and where appropriate.
Philanthropy Working Party	The PWP is an important contributor to the life of the school because it represents the school's key constituents and exemplifies philanthropic leadership. Its members provide the necessary impetus of the school's culture of philanthropy.
Staff	Staff welcome/orientation packs should contain information about philanthropy at the school. Staff: • are advocates who understand the meaning of philanthropy • support philanthropic functions when and where appropriate • ensure endowed prizes and awards are valued and promoted • recognise philanthropy as a genuine aspect of the school.

School Constituencies	Responsibilities
Parents	Parent information and enrolment packs should include philanthropic stories and the history of parent involvement at the school. Parents: • are invited to a new parent welcome function hosted each year by the PWP • are inspired to be advocates • are invited to consider matters of importance regarding the school's future • have opportunities to donate or volunteer and thus contribute to the advancement of the school • are invited to donate via voluntary contributions with fee accounts • are invited to consider making a gift for a special cause • are invited to offer their skills, wisdom or knowledge as a volunteer.
Alumni	Alumni leaders participate in the reunion program and colobratory events and offer support for the school's archives, history projects and philanthropic endeavours. Alumni: • are advocates • are engaged in hosting and organising reunions • have opportunities to contribute to the advancement of the school via the PWP • are involved in matters of importance regarding the school.

School Constituencies	Responsibilities
Past Staff	Past staff are valued by the school and invited to the presentation night and other special occasions. Their knowledge is captured and recorded at the time of leaving the school and at informal events such as fairs, reunions and celebratory events. Past staff: • are advocates • volunteer for drama or musical productions and special events • volunteer for curriculum assessment or exam invigilation • are valued contributors to school archives.
Friends	Friends include local members of parliament, local service clubs, neighbours, suppliers, past parents and grandparents. They can be connected to the school and its future through invitations to annual speech nights, school orations, ANZAC Day commemoration services or biennial fairs.

CONCLUSION

A school with a culture of philanthropy in place will receive some unexpected surprises and minor miracles. As the culture evolves, there will be many observers—those who like the school and are watching how it is progressing. They may not reveal themselves or say anything at all, but when the time is right for them, they will step forward with an impressive act of kindness or a donation that fills the room with joy.

The importance of culture to a school's operations cannot be overstated. We all understand the importance of culture in connecting people and guiding how things are done. When travelling overseas, we marvel at, enjoy and thrill in experiencing different cultures, practices, customs, food and art. And when we return home, we relax knowing we fit into the local, familiar culture. When families join a school, they should feel comfortable and relaxed in a culture that is welcoming, inclusive and positive. People should feel embraced.

CHAPTER 3

PHILANTHROPY IN SCHOOLS

If someone is described as a philanthropist, it says more about that person's values than the size of their bank balance or investment portfolio. Being wealthy is not a precursor to being philanthropic. People with considerable financial resources might make large donations, but are they being generous or philanthropic? If they are seeking recognition or notoriety because of their largesse, they may not be driven by a desire to help others or a willingness to improve the wellbeing of others. They are certainly generous but not necessarily philanthropic. If they made donations, lent their voice and were active advocates, they would assuredly be philanthropic.

Sometimes the words 'fundraising' and 'philanthropy' are used synonymously or interchangeably, implying they have the same or very similar meanings, but they are different words with different meanings. Philanthropy is relational, whereas fundraising is tactical. Fundraising is focused on securing donations, while philanthropy is focused on securing donors. Fundraising activities respond to a need, and the results are often immediate—for example, the proceeds from a raffle.

Philanthropy responds to a vision more than a need and is often prepared to take a risk by investing in a new venture or a different model. Two examples illustrating this notion come to mind. First is the investment made by donors to support medical research. Extensive trial and error and pioneering thinking are traits of researchers, and philanthropic support helps them to succeed. Another example is the range of new models being trialled that aim to reduce the incidence of homelessness. It may take longer to secure a philanthropic gift than to fundraise, but the gift is often larger and the result likely to be more effective. Table 4 below summarises the critical differences between fundraising and philanthropy.

Table 4: Fundraising or Philanthropy*

In a fundraising culture	In a philanthropic culture
Fundraising = grants from trusts or gifts from individuals and sponsorships	Philanthropy = love of humankind (lend your voice; advocacy is very potent)
It's all about the money	It's all about the relationships
Donors = money	Donors = advocacy, talent, skill, support
The focus is on big gifts	Every donation is important
Revenue generation is the responsibility of staff	Everyone in the organisation shares responsibility for income generation by serving as ambassadors and building relationships
Culture is seen as touchy-feely	Culture is an important factor in determining an organisation's effectiveness
It's all about acquiring donors	It's most important to keep donors

In a fundraising culture	In a philanthropic culture
Fundraising and engagement are siloed and have different contact lists	There is one database
Donations come first	Donations come after we engage with people
The focus is on short-term tactics like appeals and events	The focus is on the long-term benefit, which determines tactics
Fundraising is seen as an add-on	Fundraising is incorporated into and across every staff and volunteer position
Donors are contacted when there is a need or during a campaign	Donors are kept informed regularly and are thanked each year
Board and administration staff are onlookers	Board and staff have regular contact with the development office staff
The organisation functions with a scarcity mindset	The organisation has a vision and generates confidence
The organisation's leaders make decisions based on what's available	The organisation's leaders make decisions based on what its community needs
Fundraising staff are relegated to junior status	Fundraising staff are important to the organisation's overall success
Asking for money is awkward	Giving is a proud tradition
Vision, mission and goals are separate from income generation	Vision, mission and goals are aligned with income generation

*Adapted for Australian use by Gavan Woinarski from C Gibson, *Beyond Fundraising: What does it mean to build a culture of philanthropy?* Evelyn and Walter Haas Jr Fund.

Philanthropy has certain characteristics. It takes risks. It is prepared to pioneer, to be different and to try something out of the ordinary. Therefore, it creates a point of difference. It can be potent and make lasting impressions and improvements. Money is one of the vehicles that support philanthropy, but the ideas and innovations under consideration or on offer are more important than money.

Medical research and higher education are areas that depend on philanthropic and government support. Often a personal connection to a disease motivates an individual, or a group of people, to raise money to fund research. The Big Freeze at the 'G, which raises money for motor neuron disease (MND) research, is one example.

Case Study 3
Philanthropy in Medical Research

A thought-provoking CEO's attention was awakened after media reports of assaults on people who were hit from behind without warning. When the victims of these attacks stumbled to the ground and hit their head on the hard pavement, extensive swelling of the brain occurred which could result in death. The CEO set about finding a research team who could find a solution and discovered a group led by a neurologist based at Cambridge University's teaching hospital, Addenbrooke, which was focused on how to rapidly reduce the brain swelling that can be fatal after such trauma. The researchers identified an out-of-patent cancer drug as a possible remedy for swelling of the brain, and the philanthropist CEO financed the necessary research. A drug is now being trialled in the United Kingdom and Australia. The research has an eight-year time line and is in its third year. A solution could be found in our lifetime.

Case Study 4
Philanthropy in Higher Education

The chairman of a large private nationwide company believes in positive psychology—that an optimistic and positive outlook and demeanour can influence how a person behaves and thinks. He invests in his staff and prefers to say there are no problems, just opportunities and different solutions. He spent about six years working with a university to develop a unit of study in positive psychology, and the goal was to have all undergraduates at the university study this unit. The underlying premise was that positive psychology is a worthy topic to know about and practise rather than just a catchphrase. The university now includes this unit for all its undergraduates to study.

The stories above underline the belief that philanthropy should take risks, pioneer and think outside the square. These individual acts have been to the benefit of many people and did not necessarily involve large amounts of money. They came from a vision for a better world, and I believe they are philanthropic. Such philanthropists see a bigger picture where a group, or person, deserves attention. We might call this being farsighted, where the culmination of imagination, intellect and idealism intersect. The result is something unique. It is not simply a project or a grand building, as worthy as these may be. When philanthropy is enlisted, it changes the dynamic to something larger with benefits open to many.

A school does not *need* a multimillion-dollar science wing; you can teach Year 10 chemistry in a caravan. So a capital campaign for a new science wing needs to include more than classrooms or laboratories. The new facility should aim to provide an educational experience that is a stimulating place of learning for students and staff. It should become an exemplar. Philanthropy can be enlisted to help, and philanthropists will respond if the project is truly exemplary and promotes a better future. Wisdom and experience show that philanthropy responds to a vision more than a need.

In schools, a scholarship, bursary, prize or award to support students is a fitting place for philanthropy to be engaged and a good place to begin building an enduring culture of philanthropy. In this section, scholarships, bursaries, prizes and awards will be referred to collectively as honours. Honours are student-focused, have the future in mind and are for the benefit of many. If they are endowed, they will provide a benefit for many years to come. Donors and bequestors are often motivated by the idea of an honour endowed in their name. This notion will be explored later in this chapter, but first we need to explore some practicalities.

In Chapter 2, I proposed a new operational model aimed at building an enduring culture of philanthropy in schools. It involves merging the three main subgroups of a school into one entity. These three groups are parents, alumni and the foundation. This new model prevents these three subgroups from operating in silos and promotes an understanding among members about each group's purpose and what they want to achieve. For example, alumni may be interested in forming sporting sections, hosting reunions and offering career advice. Some members of the parents' group may be alumni and so could offer advice or suggestions to the alumni group. Over time, there will be a growing understanding of each subgroup's programs and what resources the school needs to allocate for each group to thrive. It becomes more about 'us' and less about 'me'. Collective understanding grows and with it teamwork and an appreciation of the role each group plays in the school's overall community relations context.

A school may have a foundation or a similar body to promote giving. Often when people hear the word 'foundation', a common response is to look away. If a whole group understands that acquiring donors is more important than getting donations—donors are people, part of humankind—there is a monumental shift in how people perceive seeking gifts.

The parents' group may want to host the annual dinner, oration, fair and Mother's Day and Father's Day breakfasts. These are perfect activities for such a group. If parents organising these events are part of a bigger group, they will appreciate input from other sections of the school community in defining the event's purpose and then planning and hosting the events.

Along the way, the importance of hearing different ideas becomes apparent and there is greater understanding of how collecting data adds to the overall reach of community relations. Hosting an event is not just preparing name tags and a menu. Collecting data for the school's customer relationship management (CRM) database is also important. If a school knows who comes to its events, it knows who to connect with and thank. Those attending events may be donors, alumni or current or future parents. The intersections can be revealing and are more likely to happen if everyone is sensitive to the comprehensive nature of community relations. The key elements of a strong culture of philanthropy in a school are summarised in Appendix 1.

PHILANTHROPY WORKING PARTY

For the purposes of this book, the new operating model will be called the Philanthropy Working Party (PWP). Before this group is launched in the school community, terms of reference and a set of meeting guidelines need to be developed. The terms of reference should detail why the PWP exists, what its purpose is and the school's expectations for the group. The meeting guidelines should describe how the PWP will operate, how its members should behave, and their roles and responsibilities. The guidelines and terms are important because they give prospective and current PWP members an understanding of the group's operational structure and remit. They will help people decide if they would like to be involved and help establish a purposeful culture for the group from the outset. For example, the guidelines might stipulate that members have a maximum five-year tenure. This helps prevent the group from being 'owned' by a few and fosters renewal. Such controls and parameters give confidence to prospective members that the PWP has a clear purpose and will not be a talkfest.

The terms of reference ensure there are clear demarcations so the PWP is not sidetracked by excursions into school management or trivia. The meeting guidelines stipulate that PWP members are expected to read and consider the contents of meeting notes (minutes), briefing papers and reference documents in a timely manner. They are also expected to contribute to the overall objectives of the PWP in a collegiate manner and conduct themselves in an open-minded fashion. Sample PWP terms of reference and meeting guidelines are provided in Appendix 2 and Appendix 3 respectively.

Members of the PWP should be drawn from the different constituencies of the school. The ratio will vary according to a school's history with its constituents and the intimacy of its connection with them. As an example, the PWP could have as a minimum three alumni, four parents, one past staff member, two current staff members, a board member and the principal as ex officio. The board member could be the chair, thus adding gravitas to the PWP and clearly demonstrating support from the board and principal for the PWP's objectives. The ideal number of PWP members is more than 12 and less than 20. Volunteers have personal and professional commitments that mean there will always be some absentees at a meeting. Too few people—less than 12—makes the group look exclusive to outsiders. Staff, alumni and parents talk, so the more connected, positive advocates you can recruit, the better. One of philanthropy's best partners is the voice; the positive voice sends good messages. The more advocates, the better the end result.

Some schools will already have in place a parents' group and/or an alumni association. These two groups may see the arrival of the PWP as a threat that will lead to the eventual dilution of their purpose and status. The school executive may see the introduction of this new model as upsetting the applecart, and there may be a perception that there is a risk of getting the current group of volunteers offside. However, in reality establishing a PWP is all about bringing people together. This is where leadership can play a vital role. The PWP is about everyone working in concert rather than in separate groups assembling their own following. The school's leaders can take the time to position the new structure and reinforce its benefits. There may be a few awkward months, but no more, because once people see the power of collective endeavour, any concerns become yesterday's news.

The board should have philanthropy as an agenda item at every meeting. The PWP should provide a written report to the board twice a year outlining the PWP's progress, achievements and priorities. Such a report reminds the board the PWP exists and is functioning well.

A modest budget can be allocated for the PWP to cover the cost of catering for meetings and any incidentals. The school can provide the PWP with a meeting place on campus and cover the costs associated with security, cleaning and printing. Some human resources will need to be given to help the PWP manage its events and to update the website to include stories and messages about philanthropy in its community relations section. Including the school's archivist in PWP event planning is respectful and very useful.

BENEFIT FUND

The word 'foundation' is often used to describe a school's fundraising department. It can be the name of a legal entity or simply a vehicle to promote giving. It has certain connotations and can conjure an idea in people's minds that it is all about money. An alternative to a foundation is a benefit fund. The word 'benefit' has a clearer meaning than 'foundation' and a contemporary rather than a traditional feel. When establishing a giving program, using the descriptor 'benefit fund' makes it clear that gifts are placed in a separate fund to provide a benefit.

> **Case Study 5**
> **Values-based Giving**
>
> A school is planning its 40th birthday, and one part of its celebrations will be to seek gifts to endow prizes for students who exemplify the school's values. Every community member will be asked for a $40 gift for the future fund. This is a reasonable sum that should attract many donors and therefore prompt many thank-you receipts. Seeking gifts to support the school's values will appeal to a different audience compared to the traditional method of seeking gifts for something material.

Schools can establish various legal entities enabling them to seek donations and offer a tax deduction. Schools can solicit tax-deductible donations from four vehicles: a public ancillary fund (PuAF) known as a deductible gift recipient (DGR), including item 1 or item 2; a scholarship fund; a building fund; and a library fund. Each requires its own constitution and trust deed, set of policies, annual auditing, annual reporting to the ACNC and a trustee. The school is usually the trustee. Each fund will have its own set of accounts and bank accounts that are separate from the school's accounts. This is a good point to stress to a school's community because it can dispel the notion that gifts just go into an operating account or a big black hole. Recruiting community members to serve as directors or to volunteer on a committee of these entities is a useful way to engage the school's constituents in philanthropic ventures. These people will gain knowledge and be active advocates of philanthropy and the school.

Schools with a PuAF can secure gifts from many sources: individuals, private ancillary funds (PAFs), trusts and foundations, corporations, the public and overseas grant makers. A PuAF could be a useful vehicle to secure funds for an innovative program a school would like to implement that is funded by a foundation or corporation. For example, a program could be in the area of teacher professional development; a teaching fellowship or a pilot program to examine the merits of a new Year 9 curriculum. The point here is that donations do not always have to be about something tangible or be made by individuals. Donations can be accumulated to form an endowment fund or accumulated over some months before they are used to fund a particular purpose. For example, a year's worth of voluntary contributions to the building fund may be kept aside and used to upgrade classrooms during the summer break. A gift submission template for formulating submissions to PAFs, trusts and foundations can be found in Appendix 7.

Schools should inform donors how their donations will be used and the benefits their donations have provided. Sharing this information in periodical reports (such as newsletters or monthly emails) helps build confidence that donations are used for the benefit of students and not to subsidise the school's running costs.

Hosting an annual donor and volunteer thank-you function is an important duty of the PWP and the school. This occasion is a good opportunity to explain how donations improved the learning outcomes for students and a good forum for the school's leaders to personally thank donors and promote philanthropy. Such events mix two very important subgroups: donors and volunteers.

At one donor and volunteer thank-you event, I noticed the principal in conversation with a Year 7 parent. There were smiles all round. After the event, the principal shared the essence of this conversation with me. It was the parent's first year at the school, and her family's first experience of an independent education. She felt her $50 donation was too small and she did not deserve to be thanked for it. The principal explained that her donation would be combined with other similar donations and the end result would be very useful. The parent resolved to keep on giving. Every donation of money, time or resources is important and should be thanked and acknowledged. An example of thanking guidelines for a school is provided in Appendix 12.

ENDOWMENT FUND

Spending every donation is laudable, but there is an alternative to consider. Creating an endowment fund is a persuasive way to inspire donors. It is something that is unusual but innovative and therefore has a particular appeal.

Case Study 6
The Power of Endowment

The widow of an alumnus wanted to do something special in memory of her husband. She knew he loved his old school, but she was not sure what to do or how to go about it. She told one of her late husband's schoolmates that she would like to explore making a gift to his alma mater that would carry his name. At first, she was thinking about creating a biology prize, because he was a surgeon and dux of his medical cohort. After many conversations and visits, she came to realise a scholarship bearing his name would be ideal, but the sum needed to endow a scholarship was far more than she had thought. It was within her means but could have compromised her future. A more fitting solution entailed making a bequest to endow an academic scholarship in her husband's name, and she made a modest donation in the meantime. This decision had two noticeable benefits. It did not change her bank balance and her story could be shared with the wider community, especially her husband's cohort. The results were impressive. Enquiries slowly came in from different constituents, alumni, past staff and current parents seeking information about endowing prizes, scholarships and awards. Another alumna from her husband's year was motivated to endow a music scholarship.

Table 5 below demonstrates how an endowment fund works. Actuaries tell us to assume a return on invested funds of 5 per cent per annum. Financial houses usually return CPI + 3 per cent, which in today's world is about 5.5 per cent. In the 2021 calendar year many investment houses returned 8.2 per cent. The tax status of an endowment fund means it does not pay tax on investment income and receives the benefits of franking credits. Table 5 shows the investment returns on different amounts. A small amount is added to the corpus each year so the fund's capacity is not eroded by inflation. A modest administration fee is deducted to meet the cost of professional advice to manage the fund. However, it is prudent to remember that endowments will suffer a one in nine year loss.

Table 5: How an Endowment Fund Could Operate

Sum	Annual Return (5%)	Distribution (90% of the return)	Administration	Return to Corpus
$5,000	$250	$225	$10	$15
$10,000	$500	$450	$10	$40
$50,000	$2,500	$2,250	$20	$230
$200,000	$10,000	$9,000	$50	$950
$400,000	$20,000	$18,000	$50	$1,950
$1,000,000	$50,000	$45,000	$50	$4,950

The endowment fund might be called the future fund. This name indicates its purpose and is a departure from the usual description. A school can manage its future fund in a conservative manner using bank term deposits or a fixed interest term offered by other investment institutions. This strategy is capital guaranteed but does not make the fund grow. Once the fund has accumulated more than $500,000 the money should be managed by a professional funds manager. Such organisations will levy a modest fee for non-profit organisations and charities. Given it will generate much higher returns than term deposits and fixed-interest options, this option is worth considering. The bottom line with investments is to focus on the net return, not the size of the fees.

ANNUAL APPEAL

An annual appeal is an appeal that seeks a modest gift from the main constituents of a school: its alumni, past staff, current staff and current parents. Neighbours, local businesses and local councils, who are environmental stakeholders, are not included. The concept of an annual appeal originated in the United States, where its primary purpose was to raise money for a school's teaching staff because they receive modest salaries. For example, the starting salary for a Year 10 maths teacher in Kentucky is about $56,000 per annum, and the average salary for a teacher in Texas is $58,000. The annual appeal's income helps augment teacher salaries. In Australia the focus has shifted from supporting staff salaries to supporting particular projects.

Requests to support an annual appeal can be distributed in a number of ways. They can be emailed or posted or appear as an online option on the school's website. The communication channels used depend on the cause, the relevance of the appeal to the intended donor group and the strength of the relationship with that group. Connections with current parents might be made via the weekly email, for example. Young alumni might be inspired by a story posted on social media. More senior alumni might receive a letter and donation form in the mail. A sample donation/pledge form is provided in Appendix 8.

Provided there is a plan and the cause has been researched and is known to appeal to prospective donors, annual appeals can be worthwhile. Research is important. Too often a school's leaders discuss and then decide what the project or cause might be, yet they forget to ask the most important group, the potential donors. If the potential donors are consulted and enlisted, the appeal is likely to have a better result than if they were ignored. Parents might want to support a different project to alumni or past staff, and this is good. Each constituency will have its preferences, and the ease of modern communication channels provides opportunities to craft messages that are specific to each group at a modest cost.

The following three examples show variations on an annual appeal. Each has its own purpose with different intended results.

- **Example A:** Aim to have five donors make a $1,000 commitment before the appeal opens. Prospective donors are then invited to make a $100 gift that will be matched by the five donors recruited initially, with the intention of recruiting 100 donors. Some donations will be at the $50 level, others at $200. The important element here is recruiting leaders who provide tangible proof that this is a project worth supporting. The pre-campaign messages and subsequent communications can engender support, especially if people are regularly informed of the appeal's progress. The voice of a donor is very potent, so the more donors, the better.

- **Example B:** Launch an appeal seeking a modest ($50) gift from all the cohorts that enjoyed a reunion during the year. Messaging can happen at the reunion/s emphasising the idea that the school is seeking modest gifts and would like to thank as many donors as possible.
- **Example C:** Connect and inspire a particular subgroup with whom the school has a specialised engagement plan, such as scientists, doctors, builders or past students involved in the annual school drama production. For example, the school's annual appeal may be directed to those interested in the sciences and seek 50 gifts of $100 to endow an annual science prize.

A voluntary contribution is a sum added to each term's fee account. Donors can choose between donating to the scholarship, library or building fund. There is always tension between the desire to raise funds and the need to acquire donors. Asking for a large sum reduces the likelihood of people donating. Acquiring donors is more important than raising money. A voluntary contribution of $50 is reasonable, and such a modest sum should prompt more donations than a request for $150. As a result, more people can be invited to the annual donor thank-you function.

At the beginning of each year, information should be sent to donors and all current parents detailing how the previous year's donations were used, even if this information was shared at the annual donor thank-you function. In this way, everyone is informed about how donations have improved learning. Reporting back to donors shows faith in the process of seeking gifts and then delivering. An example receipt letter from a principal is provided in Appendix 9.

A giving day is a specific day each year dedicated to securing donations, allowing for plenty of planning, preparation and preliminary messaging. Giving days can secure many gifts, and therefore generate the need to write many thank-you notes. A school may consider hosting an annual giving day that coincides with founders' day or another auspicious date for the school.

Pleasant surprises do happen. A school that is 20 years old with an average enrolment of 800 students will have in its database the names and contact details of thousands of past and current staff, students, parents and board members. It is safe to assume there would be about 7,000 names in such a school's database. Experience suggests there would be about 250 people who have a very fond connection to the school. Of these 250 people, a dozen could be prospective major donors and about 10 could be potential bequest prospects.

> **Case Study 7**
> **Share the Story**
>
> In one instance, a past staff member, a teacher of English, contacted the school to offer her congratulations for using the correct definition of philanthropy. After several meetings, she offered to establish an endowed, named prize for English. She shared her story with current staff and with the school's community. This encouraged dialogue and others to come forward with a similar proposal.

A well-managed database can reveal hidden gems. Data collected from voluntary contributions and annual appeals can be analysed to reveal prospective donors and trends. Over the years it may become evident that the school community responds to appeals focused on academic and cultural pursuits more than sport. Such information helps guide the direction of future appeals. Sharing this information with the PWP can solicit excitement about future possibilities. Donors who give every year are indicating they have loyalty to and an affinity for the school. Current parents who are both alumni and donors are truly connected. Past staff who give are likely to be bequest prospects. Ignoring data means lost opportunities.

Case Study 8
Fill in the Gaps

One school was preparing for its 40th birthday celebrations. It knew its alumni data was incomplete and there were some discrepancies. A call for help via social media channels and at reunions helped fill these gaps and found many missing alumni. One alumna replied, 'I have never given because I have never been asked'. Another said, 'Please leave me alone'.

These examples of alumni feedback are helpful pieces of information because they let you know where you stand and help avoid future mistakes. After all, not everyone liked their school days or would attend a reunion. Maybe the person who has never been asked could be a signatory to an annual appeal. A trained and dedicated staff member responsible for the database will always avoid misplaced communication and pay dividends.

Case Study 9
The Importance of Connection

A Melbourne independent school received a $6 million bequest from a past student who was not a donor. He attended the school for four years, and very little was known about him. His name did not appear on any honour board or prize list. Over the years, he had moved locations but always kept the school informed of his current address. He attended a 50-year reunion, and informal anecdotes from that event indicated few of his cohort knew much about him. However, he had an affection for his old school, as his bequest testifies. The executors of his estate informed the school it was essentially a thank-you gift to the school because the education he received set him up for a successful life. His bequest was to establish a fund to be invested in perpetuity. The income is used to pay for tuition fees for students in necessitous circumstances. Twenty-two years later, this fund is still working and has supported more than 60 students since its inception.

Similar stories can be found in many schools, and newer independent schools will likely receive a surprise in the future from an unexpected source provided they keep in contact with their constituents. The key is regular communication about the school's constant evolution, including stories about students, donors and other curious anecdotes.

CAPITAL CAMPAIGN

Many principals are keen to run a capital campaign to raise money to help pay for a particular physical asset. Preparation is the key to success. The campaign should focus on securing enough gifts to reach the target. Schools should bear in mind that the promotion of major gifts and naming rights can distance people who do not have the financial capacity to make a large gift but would still like to make a gift they are proud of, no matter the size. A capital campaign needs to ensure that the school's stakeholders understand all gifts are important, as illustrated in Table 6 below.

Another point to keep front of mind is describing gifts as generous. We do not know the financial details or family circumstances of our donors, so how can we describe a gift as generous? A gift of $50,000 may be impressive and much needed by the campaign committee, but is it generous? The donor may have given such a sum ensuring it did not constrain their family's personal lifestyle or be financially threatening. In other words, it was a comfortable gift to make—maybe not generous, but certainly appreciated.

It is generally agreed that when conducting a capital campaign, major gifts total about 85 per cent of the overall goal. It is recommended that the major gifts should be secured as pledges or donations before the public announcement of the campaign to all of the school's stakeholders. But here is a point of difference to consider. In Chapter 2 the virtues of an enduring culture of philanthropy were promoted and explained. In such a culture, philanthropy is spoken about and acknowledged and its true meaning is familiar to students and adults. When celebrating the announcement of the campaign, why not mention an array of different donors? Could the school captain make the announcement and mention that the Year 12s have made a donation? Perhaps consider securing gifts from the youngest alumni and the oldest alumni, thus showing that everyone is included. Millennials like to feel valued and have shown they are wiling donors, so involve them. These approaches shift the emphasis from securing gifts from people who have an obvious capacity to give to a more inclusive philanthropic culture. Schools should promote and acknowledge that a modest gift of $100 is welcomed and valued.

MAJOR GIFTS

A major gift is a contribution made by an individual, family or corporation that is a significant amount for the donor and the school. A major gift is often customised for the donor and aimed for a specific project or program area. Many schools start with a definition of a major gift at five to ten times the annual gift range. For some, a major gift may be $1,000; for others it may be $10,000.

When done right, major gifts are an incredibly cost-effective way to raise money. Running a successful major gifts program takes a lot of critical thinking and tenaciousness, but it is certainly a lot less work than adding another event such as a gala ball or golf day to an overcrowded calendar. Major gifts are a more sustainable way to do funding than transactional models like grant applications and direct mail. The longer you work with donors and the more they give, the easier it is to secure future gifts from repeat donors and new donors.

Cost effectiveness can also be managed against staff costs. An employee dedicated to major gift fundraising over a two-year period might cost $230,000 and raise $1 million. Investing $230,000 and getting back $1.2 million inside 24 months is a good return, especially when compared to investing this sum in a term deposit at 0.9 per cent, which would return $20,700.

Major gifts can be deposited into the building fund for buildings, equipment or resources or to the scholarship fund, which provides income support for honours such as scholarships, bursaries, prizes and awards. Donations to the library fund can be used to purchase learning resources.

Major gifts are secured following a period of relationship building between the school and its prospective major donors. This phase should take at least 18 months, though the time depends on the scale of the gifts being sought, the depth of interest of the prospective donors and their connection to the school. In a capital campaign scenario, an important motivator will be the focus of the campaign—for example, performing arts, sport, STEM etc. Some prospective donors may not like the project for a sports pavilion and therefore make a modest gift. However, in five years' time they could be very excited to support a new drama theatre. Always keep people connected.

Because donors have different motivations, interests and passions for giving, a school should maintain relations with all of its constituencies. Maintaining relationships is stewardship. It is important and should not be put aside, because it is a cornerstone of community relations. There are many examples of surprise gifts that seemed to come out of the blue. The co-founder of Nike, Philip Knight, made two large donations to Stanford University. In 2016 he donated $400 million to fund scholarships. In 2022 he and his wife, Penny, gave $75 million to fund research into neurodegenerative brain conditions such as Parkinson's and Alzheimer's diseases. Knight graduated with an MBA from Stanford in 1962; Stanford kept in touch with him for 54 years and reaped a substantial reward.

A capital campaign's success is determined by its leaders endorsing a clearly articulated vision that supports the rationale for the campaign. It follows detailed research about the merits of the proposal that is supported by evidence and intellect. Highly polished sentences and pretty pictures are not enough. A school's leaders should demonstrate their commitment to the campaign by making their own donation and allocating resources to support the campaign. When leaders lend their voice, are advocates and make time in their diaries to connect with potential donors, this work is highly visible and success will follow.

A capital campaign has two aims: to raise money and to recruit donors. Table 6 below indicates two variations of a capital campaign with the same dollar goal. There are merits to both approaches. Campaign A means fewer people will have to be managed and cultivated for a gift. Campaign B means there is much more activity to be managed but many more donors will be recruited. The 599 donors are certainly advocates, which means there will be many stories to collect and share and lots of thank-you notes to deliver.

Table 6: Capital Appeal Campaign Comparison

Campaign A aim: $1 million		Campaign B aim: $1 million	
2 × $250,000	$500,000	2 × $100,000	$200,000
2 × $100,000	$700,000	2 × $50,000	$300,000
5 × $10,000	$750,000	20 × $10,000	$500,000
10 × $5,000	$800,000	25 × $5,000	$625,000
50 × $2,000	$900,000	100 × $2,000	$825,000
100 × $1,000	$1,000,000	200 × $500	$925,000
		250 × $200	$975,000
Donors: 169	Total: $1,000,000	Donors: 599	Total: $975,000

Many school principals feel nervous about investing in philanthropy because the lead time is long and the results are slow to materialise. The receipt book should not be the driver, though. It is the vision, delivered by the leaders, that counts.

School principals may choose to consult with an outside agency to help with its philanthropy, communications or anything else. A MOU template is provided as Appendix 5.

Donor quotes

> *'I am happy to make a gift because lots of students will benefit.'*
>
> *'This is not about money; it is about fulfilling a vision.'*
>
> *'Others have given in the past; now it is our turn.'*
>
> *'Go and experience what it feels like in your bones to do something for others, then remember that feeling.'*

The following steps outline the process for securing donations:

- **Step 1: Identification.** Who are the people who are likely and have the capacity to make a large donation, based on their ability to give, interest in the cause and depth of connection to your school?
- **Step 2: Discovery.** The discovery process is often compared to a first date. This is your chance to learn more about the potential donor and their interests. In conversation discover which projects or programs your prospect may want to learn more about.
- **Step 3: Cultivation.** This is the process of building a relationship that engenders mutual respect and knowledge about one another, which enables you to ask for a gift.
- **Step 4: Asking.** Ask a donor to make a gift for a particular purpose. Often there are some back-and-forth conversations about the gift, including the size of the gift. Will it be a single contribution or a pledge over time? At this stage major donors often ask if others give at this level. This is a golden opportunity to ask other prospective donors to connect and inspire them to join this donor to maximise giving. At this point you can explain to the major donor that their gift will attract similar gifts—that is, it will be a multiplier.
- **Step 5:** Confirmation, thanking and receipting. This is best done personally, because a shake of the hand is stronger than an exchange of emails.
- **Step 6:** Stewardship. Maintain a relationship by showing donors the impact of their gift. This is effectively reporting back and being faithful to your organisation and the donor that the gift has been used wisely. After you have successfully stewarded the donor, it is time to assess if they are ready to be inspired to help in other ways.

Prospective donors are not created equal. To prioritise connecting with your identified prospective donors, it is best to assess them based on the following two criteria:

1. where the potential donor falls on the donor commitment continuum
2. the financial capacity of the donor.

The relationship between these two areas will indicate the priority level you should assign to the donor.

Appendix 13 outlines the donor commitment continuum. This is the staged development of a donor from ignorance to involvement and finally ownership.

When assessing the financial capacity of potential donors, we should bear in mind that someone with moderate capacity now may have greater capacity later; thus, the value of stewardship. The priority grid in Figure 1 below is a simple tool to use when researching and segmenting your database.

Figure 1: Database Research and Priority Grid*

	Financial capacity: High	
	B Medium priority: focus on developing commitment to the organisation	**A** High priority: focus on major gift opportunities
	D Low priority: do not focus your efforts here for major gifts; maybe bequests	**C** Medium priority: maintain engagement and celebrate initial gifts
	Interest: Low → High	

*Source: Advancement Resources (USA), founded by Joe Golding

In summary, the continuum, priority grid and the six steps detailed above provide the framework for a school to secure gifts. If the framework is applied with respect and care, and within an overarching philanthropic approach, schools should feel capable to run their own successful campaigns.

BEQUESTS

A bequest is a gift to a person, group or organisation that comes after a person has passed away. The direction and explanation of the bequest are included in the person's will or added as a codicil to that will. Sample bequest wording and a codicil template can be found in Appendix 10 and Appendix 11 respectively. A bequest is usually the largest gift a person makes, so bequests should form part of a school's philanthropic program. For a school, the most likely bequestors are alumni, past staff and bereaved current parents.

> **Case Study 10**
> **A Treasured Award**
>
> At one school, a family made a gift to support the annual drama production. This was a gift of several thousand dollars in memory of the family's child who died soon after leaving school. Fifteen years later, the award is treasured and the family is included in the opening night of each year's drama production.

A popular and proven vehicle to promote and secure bequests is a bequest society. A bequest society is established to thank and acknowledge people in their lifetime; after all, you can acknowledge but not thank a deceased person. A bequest society can carry a name that has a particular resonance and connection to the school's history—for example, the name of a notable school landmark or the name of the first chair or principal. Melbourne Grammar School's bequest society is called the Witherby

Tower Society because the Witherby clock tower is a dominant part of the school's skyline. Methodist Ladies' College in Melbourne has the Stella Argenta bequest society in recognition of the school's emblem, the silver star.

Bequestors will want to know what is possible and how their bequest will be used. Do they want their bequest to recarpet room 3, or is there a better option? A bequest society is a useful vehicle for explaining how a bequest can be invested to advance your school. A bequest could be used to establish a prize, an award, a scholarship or a bursary. Having a bequest society allows a school to promote bequests and tell future bequestors what is possible.

The bequest society can explain in its literature, on a website and at functions how much is needed to endow a bursary or an academic prize, for example. In general terms, an endowment to support an academic prize or a service award could be $5,000. Endowing a full scholarship or bursary depends on the school's fees. A $400,000 gift would produce $20,000 in income each year; a teaching fellowship to support professional development might be $100,000, generating $5,000 per year. Securing bequests in an endowment fund is a good message to give future bequestors, because bequests are promoted as lifelong gifts that will provide a benefit for students well into the future. A template for a Memorandum of Gift to establish a perpetual endowment is provided in Appendix 4.

Some people make a bequest to a school for a bursary or scholarship, but the sum provided is not sufficient. The bequestor may have settled on the sum without contacting the school; they were just following a gut feeling. Having a bequest society enables a school to inform and inspire its community about the sums needed to endow honours and improve the lives of others. It is about the love of humankind.

The introduction to this book includes a story about a couple who lived in the Riverina area of southern New South Wales. During a visit with the couple, I came to understand that the husband had been a boarder with his brother and they both loved their school days. The distance from home to school meant each journey to and from school took nearly two days with an overnight stay in Albury. During the Second World War they both enlisted in the RAAF and trained as bomber pilots. On a return mission from a night raid over Germany, his brother's plane was destroyed. Some 40 years later, when it came to making a bequest, he was adamant he would like to establish a scholarship for a boarder in his brother's name at their alma mater. The school was pleased and proud to accept this proposal. Eventually, after the husband and wife had passed on, the school received sufficient funds to fully endow two boarding scholarships.

Another story relates to a school founded 30 years ago. A staff member was diagnosed with a terminal illness. This was her first professional appointment, and she loved her job as a Grade 2 teacher. She made a bequest as a thank-you gift because the school had given her the first opportunity to pursue a career that was the love of her life.

Bequest societies have been used with considerable success in schools. A bequest society needs a modest staffing allocation in the beginning— about 0.2 EFT. Depending on the depth of connection between the school and its potential bequestors, it may take two years to establish and about four years to reap rewards. As time passes, messages at reunions and stories in school publications will generate enormous goodwill and several bequests.

CONCLUSION

Each school has its own unique feeling. This feeling is the result of the school's history, location, demography, religious affiliation (if any), philosophy and accumulated successes, and it influences the school's modus operandi. It is not a static state of affairs; there is a continuous evolution taking place. Provided the origins of the school's foundation are respected, each school will develop to meet the contemporary needs of its students.

We all appreciate and understand that a school's existing employees and board members are the current custodians of the school. They have managerial and governance issues to manage and execute, but they should not lose sight of the importance of culture. An enduring culture of philanthropy would be an impressive legacy for the current group of leaders to leave behind and might well outlast the renovations to the science laboratory.

CHAPTER 4

FUNDRAISING IN SCHOOLS

The noisy and excited sounds heard on a school fair day create many happy memories. Music, yelps, cheering voices and the clickety-clack of the spinning wheel are some of the sounds so many of us can recall. There are numerous activities to enjoy: pony rides, fairy floss, lucky dips, the merry-go-round, giant slides and painted faces. There is something for everyone—children, parents, grandparents—and good times can be had by all.

On the Friday before an annual school fair, I remember seeing students lined up at lunchtime to buy their tickets and make pacts with their buddies about where and when to meet. Nearby, parents were erecting tents, plugging in the coolroom and setting up various stalls. The school grounds had been transformed with bunting, signs and banners. Areas reserved for teaching and learning became homes for white elephant, bric-a-brac and second-hand book stalls. A colourful and merry atmosphere was heightened by music beating across the campus.

School fairs have logistical and people challenges, but these are counterbalanced by numerous benefits. They create great connections, involve many people, get results quickly and can enhance the reputation of the school within its neighbourhood and local community. They bring new people to your school and are therefore a potent marketing tool.

Fundraising activities in schools provide numerous opportunities to engage students, staff, parents and alumni. Fundraising events bring people together with a common cause in mind. As a result, they often foster friendships, new connections for the school and the possibility of future partnerships. Fundraising can provide money for projects identified by staff, students or parents. Because it is *their* project, it will be successful. Results are quick to materialise, so there is a great sense of achievement. A Year 8 sausage sizzle, a guess the number of jelly beans in a jar competition, a cupcake stall—all of these fun activities will raise money. Importantly, they also provide experiences in planning, teamwork, profit and loss, and risk and reward. They use few resources, have modest outlays and are largely adult free, so they are very appealing to students.

There are some fundamentals of fundraising in a school. The activities and the cause must not conflict with the values of the school or interfere with or compromise the school's operations or reputation. The principal must be informed and approve any proposed fundraising events or programs before planning begins. Groups associated with a school, such as Friends of Music, must seek permission before any fundraising activities and planning can begin. Similarly, the use of school premises, equipment, logo or staff needs approval in the first place. The school may provide some resources for fundraising activities—for example, paper, printing and use of facilities—but it does not underwrite success or financially contribute to the event.

Below is a summary of different fundraising activities that can involve parents, students and alumni, though maybe not all at the same time. Their extent and impact can be fashioned according to the cause, experience, age and expertise of those involved in organising such events. Each has its own strengths and weaknesses. A useful checklist to assist with organising functions and events is provided in Appendix 6.

EVENTS

Events include balls, private dinners, fairs, show-n-shines for car lovers, spelling bees, talent shows and trivia nights. These events bring together teams of volunteers who have enthusiasm and a passion for their chosen activity. Some take longer than others to plan—for example, a fair might take a committee of 20 people 12 months to plan – whereas a show-n-shine could take five people two or three months to plan and implement.

SPORTS DAYS

Activity events such as fun runs and swimathons are very good for positioning your school as health and wellbeing conscious and for bringing families and friends together. For example, fun runs can engage people of different ages in a pursuit that requires minimal organising and modest costs. Funds can be raised from entry fees and the purchase of a themed T-shirt, water bottle, hat or sunscreen. Set-up costs are modest, and if the school has sufficient space to host the event, external permissions are minimised. As a reminder, fun runs in public open spaces need local government approval before they can proceed. Bunting for the start and finish lines and a registration table are easy to organise and cheap to buy.

RAFFLES

Raffles are relatively simple to prepare and organise and are a good way to engage different people. Some people prefer to donate a prize or secure prizes from their contacts rather than being involved in the selling of tickets or being the MC at the main event. Raffle books can be purchased at a newsagency or stationer. Each state and territory has different permit requirements regarding raffles; check the consumer affairs website in your state or territory to discover the current obligations. Raffles with prizes totalling less than $5,000 can be conducted without a permit. The results of a raffle are immediate, which allows the audience to participate with applause or humorous comments—two good signs of an engaged community.

AUCTIONS

Auctions, both live and silent, are a great way to engage parents, staff, suppliers and alumni to use their networks to secure prizes. They can also be motivated to bring their friends to the event, ball or dinner dance, for example, to widen the audience for participation in the actions. Live auctions generate an exciting atmosphere when bidders bid for the heavily discounted prizes on offer. Silent auctions promote lots of interactions between bidders as they mingle along the tables displaying the goods to be sold.

CROWDFUNDING

Crowdfunding is an online experience with a short time frame—generally just weeks. It works best in response to an unexpected event, such as a tragedy or crisis. Choose the social media channel that best suits your purpose; prepare a 70- to 90-second video; build a simple website that has pictures, stories and a catchcry; and include a link to make a donation. Communicate often—maybe twice a week.

MERCHANDISE

Merchandise such as mugs, tea towels, USBs, caps etc generally have a slim profit margin and often involve high set-up and storage costs. To be successful they need constant promotion. Sometimes their appeal and shelf life can be limited. They are a good secondary marketing tool for your school if sold in high volumes.

SPECIALTY ITEMS

Often parents and alumni have an interest in speciality items such as organic produce, coffee, gourmet cakes and jams. They can be engaged in a partnership that helps the person's enterprise grow and the school to gain a share of the profits.

STANDALONE ACTIVITIES

Spinning wheels, lucky dips, lucky envelopes and tin shakes can be standalone activities run by students, alumni or parents. Primary-aged children enjoy lucky dips and lucky envelopes, crazy hair days, sausage sizzles and cupcake days.

BUSINESS SPONSORSHIP

Suppliers or local businesses can support your school with a sponsorship. Very few will offer cash, but they may offer discounts for their products or gifts-in-kind as prizes for raffles etc. Creating a formal agreement between a school and a local trader needs careful thought and is not without risks. Your school has no influence over the trader's operations, staff payments or finances. If the trader is spotlighted in the media for poor behaviour or soured relations with its staff, then your school can be adversely implicated.

FUNDRAISING AND DATA COLLECTION

There is a drawback to fundraising that we should appreciate. Participants are more or less anonymous if you collect their name only. Collecting other contact details so you can offer a thankyou after the event is prudent. Too often these activities do not require collecting a donor's contact details.

One aspect of fundraising worth exploring is the collection of information and data for the school's CRM database. In our busyness, we can overlook this important component, which is a building block of community relations. For example, three months after a school fair, volunteers, donors, suppliers etc should receive a report about how the raised funds were used and the benefits they provided. This completes the circle by explaining that the fair was for a particular purpose and that by working together 'We have delivered'.

CONCLUSION

Fundraising activities in schools are worthwhile because they connect with and involve lots of people who in turn can become advocates. An active, vocal advocate is far more potent and useful than an advertisement in a local cinema. Such activities also raise funds quickly. However, their contrast to philanthropy is worth remembering. Philanthropy involves a greater investment of time and energy over a longer period and generates much greater benefits. Both fundraising and philanthropy have their merits; the key difference is the scale of the rewards.

CHAPTER 5

COMMUNITY RELATIONS

Relationships are the cornerstones of people-centred organisations. Community relations are all about creating and managing mutually beneficial relationships. In commercial organisations, relationships are centred on sales and customer satisfaction. Customer satisfaction leads to customer loyalty and further sales.

Schools are in a unique position because their stakeholders (customers) are many and varied and each has a different origin to their connection to the school. For instance, alumni have a different connection compared to past staff or parents. This makes crafting community relations in a school variable and interesting. In essence, good community relations must be authentic and grounded in reality rather than driven by marketing embellishment. Sound relations are part of a culture of philanthropy and will underpin the school's capacity to flourish.

A school can fashion communications with a particular focus according to the group it wishes to steward. Past staff might appreciate twice yearly newsletters and an invitation to join an annual lunch. Grandparents might prefer to attend the school during a normal school day, when they can visit their grandchildren in the classroom. Current parents might prefer to be involved in student-centred activities or events that bring parents together.

Devising different activities and events to engage the various constituencies of a school community can be achieved in imaginative ways. Alumni can be connected via reunions or business breakfasts. Current parents can be connected via Mother's Day and Father's Day breakfasts, an annual fair or a more formal annual oration. Past staff can be included in the annual music concert, presentation evening or speech night and the annual open day. The style, timing and format of events to connect with a school's community members are almost limitless.

There are always 'out of the blue' occurrences when schools connect with their constituents. Wisdom and experience suggest that at least twice a year something special or unexpected will happen that is of mutual benefit. At one school I visited, a grandparent attended a tour and morning tea organised especially for grandparents. He was an electrical engineer, and a chance meeting with the principal proved that serendipity is alive and well. The school needed to assess and upgrade its electricals, and the grandparent was delighted to help. The result was a massive financial saving for the school plus the inclusion of solar power systems that minimised the school's future energy bills. As an additional benefit, the school recruited an active advocate.

A Philanthropy Working Party, as introduced in Chapter 3, is a group that represents all the main stakeholders of a school—parents, staff, past staff, alumni and grandparents. Gathering everyone into one group allows for each subset to understand the others' needs and aspirations. As a result, discussions and decisions will be based on collective knowledge and have a comprehensive basis. Collective endeavour is potent. It is worth exploring each of these constituent subgroups to gain an appreciation of their different needs, objectives and aspirations.

ALUMNI

Reunions are a popular and successful vehicle to build and maintain relations with alumni. Reunions should be cost neutral to the school on a cash basis—staff time, printing etc are the investment made by the school. Seeking payment from alumni helps ensure that people turn up to the event. If there is no payment requested, people will lack a strong commitment to attend. In such cases, bad weather or a late night out can easily deter someone from attending.

There are several aspects to reunions. First, there is the building of and/or maintaining connections. Secondly, there is the gathering of stories and memorabilia. Thirdly, there is the discovering of contact details or news of 'lost' alumni. Recruiting members of a particular cohort to help drive the reunion will help fill gaps in the database and promote attendance. Peer-to-peer relations are more potent than we often realise, so recruiting several alumni to help drive a reunion will prove beneficial.

Updating the database with current contact details or news about alumni is one aspect of information gathering. Just as important is the collecting of anecdotes and stories about past students that can be entered into a constituent's database record. Learning about alumni who have died helps a school avoid awkward moments in the future. Collecting far-ranging information expands the depth of the database and can be very useful to the archivist and any future historians who might research and write a history of the school. Also, such information can help the school with a capital appeal, because it has sourced and gathered information that gives clues about a person's or family's engagement with the school.

Organising reunions based on 10-year intervals is a formula used by many schools; five years is generally considered too often. The 10-year reunion is often scheduled away from the school with a drinks and finger-food format. The decision about where and when a 10-year reunion should take place depends on the location of the school and the postcode distribution of the cohort. The 20-, 30- or 40-year reunions should be hosted at the school. Choosing a day of the week can be problematic, but as a general rule weekends should be avoided. The 20-year and 30-year reunions can also have a drinks and nibbles format, leaving the 40-year reunion to be a lunch or dinner. It is best to consult the cohort when planning each reunion and deciding on the format, date and timing. Alternatively, a school may decide on the format and timing of reunions, which over time creates a predictable pattern. First term may be reserved for all reunions, for example.

Involving current students in reunions provides a genuine point of contact for alumni who like to share their stories of high jinks and recollections with current students. This often happens when current students accompany alumni on a tour. Students can also be incorporated in the formal part of the reunion by offering a 'welcome back to school' speech or the thankyou at the end of the reunion. When doing so, they can inform the alumni about any new aspects of the school and remind them that the traditional characteristics and familiar settings they know and remember are still in place. Current students add greater depth to the occasion and reinforce that every person has a place in the culture of philanthropy.

Organising reunions at 10-year intervals is appealing but regularly consumes valuable school resources. An alternative for schools to consider is an annual reunion day; one day of the year reserved for reunions. Having one day of the year for reunions means the school's leaders, staff, past staff and support staff can be marshalled on one day, rather than several. This day could be scheduled close to the foundation date of the school to give the occasion added gravitas. To accommodate the needs of each cohort, tours can be offered at different times and cohorts can meet in different parts of the school.

It is worth considering hosting an annual reunion day on a Saturday, starting in the late afternoon. The reunion could begin with an address by the principal at 5.30 pm in the assembly hall, followed by a Q&A session. The school captain could close proceedings by offering a thankyou to alumni for attending. Cohorts can move away to their allocated locations at 6.30 pm after the address. This idea brings people together, and the alumni will feel that there are lots of people connected to their school. It also means school resources are used for one day of the year rather than four or five. It may be sensible to 'close' the reunion at 9.30 pm, allowing time for groups to gather off site to continue their revelry.

Providing a central meet-and-greet place when hosting a reunion tends to avoid people arriving in an aimless or unsupervised manner. It also gives an opportunity for current staff or students to welcome and acknowledge people as they arrive. Another vital component of reunions is a reunion book. This is a specially bound book covered with the school's livery and embossed with the school badge, with pages inside for alumni to sign and make a comment, much like a visitors' book. Comments gathered give valuable insights about the cohort and individuals. One person might write, 'Hated the place then and still do now.' Another could comment, 'It is good to be back.' There will be other comments ranging from positive to negative. Whatever the case, it is better to know than not know. Furthermore, these comments may help indicate who might be potential bequestors, donors or active volunteers.

Following up after a reunion is critical. A simple thank-you email can be accompanied by some photos, a quote from the reunion book or a copy of the list of attendees. During the reunion there would have been the occasional humorous or odd moment and probably yelps of happiness as old friendships were rekindled. Incorporating a snippet of these moments in the follow-up ensures it is genuine and will make a lasting impression. Mention should be made of those who helped drive the reunion, including staff and volunteers. It is good to share with the cohort the number of gaps in the database that were filled because this shows that the school values its data and the help people have provided.

Older independent schools may have alumni branches in regional areas, interstate or overseas. Branch functions are good for bringing together alumni, current parents, prospective parents, grandparents and extended families. People feel valued when they are included, so inviting prospective parents, past parents and others in the circle of school friends will give branch functions an added perspective and depth of connection.

In Chapter 3, I mentioned that surprises do happen. At one school I know, a particular cohort was a close-knit group. At their reunion, it was proposed to everyone in the room that they combine their resources and make a donation each year for six years to pay half the fees of someone who would not be able to attend the school without their help. There was general agreement, but they needed to secure the support of the school for the other half of the fees. Naturally, this was forthcoming. I can report that this group is in its tenth year of offering support. Their commitment to fund a half scholarship has been shared with the general community as a good news story that echoes the philanthropic phrase, 'What can I do for others?' The subsequent goodwill and positive feelings this achievement has generated are worth more than the donations.

Schools that collect reunion data in a CRM database—rather than in an Excel sheet—and act on it will reap rewards. When the 50th, 40th or 30th anniversary celebrations come around, data can be collated and those who have attended each 10-year reunion can be personally invited. Consider championing their loyalty. There will be some pleasant surprises—among them a few handsome donations.

PAST STAFF

Past staff have viewpoints, recollections and memorabilia related to the time they served at the school. Using this knowledge allows a school to craft its messages with a particular known historical context in mind. For example, a school planning its 40th anniversary celebrations will want to connect with alumni, current and past staff who were involved in the 30th anniversary. Former staff members can add information not readily available to a school, so their involvement will add another dimension to any celebratory occasion.

Past staff members will hold memories and memorabilia that can be treasure-troves for the archivist. For this reason, consider including the archivist as an integral part of past staff gatherings. An annual get-together for past staff will slowly build connections and renew colleagues' associations forged during their time at the school. Past staff functions must include non-teaching staff. Former staff members will offer recollections and stories about a school's earlier days or a particular momentous occasion in the life of a school—for example, a fire or a flooded building.

A well-known independent school in Melbourne had a fire in its library, and after the fire was extinguished, stories of bravery and dedication emerged. Staff and students worked with energy and a sense of urgency to save what they could. A sense of teamwork was evident as they toiled to save a part of their school's history. There was no written account of this episode, so stories became myths and some misconceptions came into being. About a decade later, at a special school event to open a new library, some past staff and students returned and shared their experiences with current students and staff. Some misunderstandings were put right, and a written account was commissioned to set the record straight.

Past staff recollections can often correct stories that have grown from a casual reference into factual accounts when they are not. History can let reminiscences grow into accepted truths and become respected epic accounts; however, this is not always the case.

A final note about former staff: they are very good bequest prospects.

CURRENT STAFF

Current staff should be the school's best active advocates. Their professionalism and work ethic exhibits the school's commitment to its students' learning. Their cheerful willingness to respect the school's values is a compelling, tacit behaviour that underlines the quality of what the school represents, and what matters most.

Regular staff meetings provide a forum for administrative formalities and an opportunity for outsiders (perhaps alumni or parents) to bring new challenges and perspectives to contemporary education. Such occasions add breadth and may be a welcomed interlude to the busyness of a school term. Including contributions from alumni and current parents can be enlightening for all concerned. Current parents might make astute observations not easily seen by staff; equally, alumni can share their stories and by doing so underline the school's core values and practices.

Connecting with staff away from scheduled staff meetings is important. End-of-term drinks and/or lunches and an annual major social occasion are events that provide much-needed interactions between staff members from all sections of the school. Sometimes it might be appropriate to deliberately mix staff from different sections of the school. After all, a secondary teacher has the primary teacher to thank for teaching their pupils how to read and write.

Making the effort to mark personal celebratory moments in the lives of staff members, such as the birth of a child or an engagement, exemplifies good manners and shows sincerity. Friends and peers can make the speeches, leaving the principal to be an unspoken but active participant. Such occasions, either formal or informal, demonstrate that staff are noticed and valued.

The school board or council should consider hosting an annual function for staff where the directors can mingle with teachers and support staff. Employees will like being invited to such a function, and the idea of the board being remote and somewhat faceless will be diminished. People can swap stories, make connections and learn from one another. Staff can hear different voices and directors can give personal thanks to staff.

Soliciting comments and input from staff about different aspects of the school's operations is imperative. This participation can be achieved via subcommittees or working parties covering topics such as enrolments, facilities to support the curriculum and future directions. Despite some drawbacks, including staff in some decisions is overt and proactive. It will collect many friends and generate advocacy.

CURRENT PARENTS

Like staff and students, current parents should be the school's best active advocates. They are already engaged via their child and the associated financial investment they make. There is also the tacit trust they have given the school by enrolling their offspring.

While many parents like to organise events, others prefer to offer their skills and talents by serving on committees. Some like to share their professional expertise and experience as a board director. Whatever the case, it is important and sensible to capture and retain the interest of parents as valued volunteers. A popular vehicle to engage and oversee parents is a parents' association or parents and friends group—there are numerous names for such groups. The main purposes of these groups are to 'friendraise' and fundraise.

These groups will organise social events that bring parents and/or their children together, such as annual Mother's Day and Father's Day breakfasts. These events are organised and hosted by parents—as opposed to speech nights, ANZAC Day commemorations or valedictory events, which are hosted by the school. Parents may also like to organise a biennial fair, an annual craft display, golf day, carols on the oval—the list goes on and on. Each school will have its own preferences, and there may well be a unique event that is particular to a school that has evolved over time. One school has an annual show-n-shine, where cars are parked for onlookers to admire. It became an annual event because many of the school's families worked in the car industry, which was a major employer in the district.

An annual oration is another event that parents can organise and host in partnership with the school. This is a more formal occasion where an external guest speaker delivers an address. The oration should be challenging and thought-provoking. Senior students can join their parents to share this experience. It is a special day of the year when everyone comes together and the focus is beyond the school, because the orator will bring unfamiliar, contemporary ideas for everyone to contemplate.

Parent groups have their own politics and challenges. To avoid a parent group consuming too much of the principal's time, it is worth investing in a rigorous modus operandi. Two key documents will help a school manage its different subgroups: the terms of reference describe neatly and accurately the purpose of the subgroup and what it can and cannot do (see Appendix 2), and meeting guidelines describe how a subgroup should operate and behave and thus avoid becoming a talkfest (see Appendix 3). Before volunteers join a group, they should acknowledge that they have read, understood and will abide by the scope and recommendations of these two documents.

GRANDPARENTS

Grandparents like to be connected to the important times in the lives of their grandchildren. Inviting grandparents to an annual event when they can see their grandchildren in the school playground or classroom is heartwarming. Such events are usually centred on the early learning and primary years. Children, parents and grandparents love these days, as do staff.

CONCLUSION

A person's individual relationship with a school is a small aspect of the school's whole lifespan; however, these relationships are important because a school is the sum of all its parts. A school is an organisation always on the move, forever changing as it adapts to shifts in curriculum priorities, economic necessities, technologies and the expectations of its stakeholders. Accordingly, its relationships with its stakeholders will be evolving. There will be periods of heightened connections and emotions, such as during a major celebration, and these will wane until the next important occasion arises.

A school does not suit every student and family, and so it is normal to expect some deviation from the utopian view that everything is always rosy. Not-so-warm or unfriendly news is good news because it can be a reality check. We need to know about the not-so-good so it can be fixed. Keeping people informed, thanking and listening are the main elements of successful community relations.

CHAPTER 6

THE FUTURE OF PHILANTHROPY IN SCHOOLS

Establishing an enduring culture of philanthropy in a school will help underwrite its future and capture the hearts and minds of many people. The philanthropic culture's ultimate goal is to have people believe that giving is a proud tradition.

Philanthropy can be described as the transfer of private assets for public good. This transfer can take different forms: money, time, skills or the sharing of wisdom and experience. Motivations for such acts range from altruism to egotism. Often it is simply a willingness to help other people. The transfer of assets is not the preserve of the wealthy; anyone can participate. Philanthropy's future is bright.

The most potent motivator prompting the transfer of personal assets for the good of others is a personal connection. In the wider community, reasons motivating donors vary enormously. A passionate conservationist might make a donation to build a fence to isolate native animals from feral predators. Others may prefer to support medical research because they have had a loved one experience the impact of a disease. Some believe in creativity and so support the arts. Many donors will support a common, large-scale societal challenge, such as homelessness or domestic violence.

In schools, those most closely connected are alumni, past staff and current parents. Alumni's motivation for supporting their old school is typically derived from their interest in a particular aspect of their life as a student. Some may like to support sport, others academia, extracurricular pursuits or the professional development of teachers. Current parents might focus on improving school facilities to enhance student learning. Past staff might consider making a donation to endow a prize. We are all different, which may explain to some degree why there are more than 54,000 deductable gift recipients (DGRs) in Australia.

A building fund and scholarship fund can be promoted as different vehicles for giving that have a particular focus. Some donors will prefer to give to the building fund for capital works, equipment or upgrades to the school's infrastructure. The scholarship fund might prove attractive for those who would like to establish and endow a prize, an award, a scholarship or a bursary. All of these suggestions are student focused and have a discernible measurable benefit. Scholarships and bursaries are two causes that will attract donors, because they are people centric and future focused. If their donation is endowed, thus providing long-term benefits, donors know their gift will keep on giving for many years to come. 'In perpetuity' is a handsome phrase that can prove to be a worthy incentive for prospective donors.

All schools have unique attributes. One school might find it can secure donations for outdoor education resources, and another school might attract donations for astronomy because it has an observatory equipped with telescopes. A boarding school may promote boarding scholarships. Newer independent schools might seek support for new facilities to improve their capacity to deliver a broad education or a particular curriculum innovation. Schools should capitalise on their points of difference and think outside the square.

About a decade ago, one of a school's loyal families was asked to make a large donation for an aquatic centre. The prospective donors did not like the idea and challenged the school to think sideways. 'Isn't there something better than an indoor heated swimming pool?' they asked. The result was the creation of a health and wellbeing centre that houses a swimming pool, gymnasium, and exercise and pilates rooms. It is staffed by sports coaches, psychologists and a nutrition expert. This resource has proved useful and popular with staff and students. It was an innovative venture that became a noticeable point of difference.

One aspect of philanthropy that is often overlooked is its willingness to pioneer. The world is changing, and innovative ventures are attractive. Here are two examples. The first is an endowed teaching fellowship. Teachers are a school's best resource. Parents know this, and the COVID-19 pandemic has emphasised the importance of teaching in the development and education of our youngsters. Staff will feel valued and be more proactive about building an enduring culture of philanthropy if a teaching fellowship is part of the mix. The school's professional development budget could be added to the income from the endowment fund, and the combined sum could be impressive. The second example is to involve parents, students and staff in creating an entrepreneurs' fund. Students often have imaginative ideas that languish because of a lack of funds or resources. If staff and students combine their enthusiasm, supporters could be inspired to fund an annual award to reward and help implement good ideas emanating from the classroom rather than the executive team.

If we shift our attention away from schools to the wider community, it is evident that philanthropy is gaining a greater profile and understanding within the mainstream population. We hear stories about people pledging to give away much of their wealth during their lifetime and reports of large donations being made to medical research institutes, universities and for the environment and wildlife. The most noticeable aspect of these gifts is the involvement of the donor in the project or cause.

Traditional philanthropy involved organisations connecting with and wooing prospective donors, hoping to secure a gift. The efforts were generally focused on board members, trustees of foundations or the matriarch or patriarch of affluent families. Established relationships and the reputation and status of the organisation seeking a gift were seen as important ingredients to inspire a donation. It was all about oiling an existing network and connecting with known people; newcomers were rarely seen. Things have changed.

In our contemporary world, donors want to become more involved; they want to be around the decision-making table and be part of the planning of any appeal or program. They prefer the interactions and relationships to be less transactional and more personal. They are asking, 'What impact will my gift make?' This thinking is pronounced among millennials and younger technology executives. Their support will come once the achievable outcomes are clearly articulated and they are engaged. If we transpose this mindset to the school context, we can adjust our thinking to match the contemporary world. In schools, the executive team might prepare a briefing paper about a major fundraising appeal to go to the board for final approval. Once approved, plans and actions start. The pieces missing in the formulation of the plan are the main stakeholders, such as donors, staff, current parents and alumni. Seeking input, and thus buy-in, from stakeholders to help shape the briefing paper is beneficial.

Millennials regard access to education as a top priority. The children of migrants and refugees have a similar view. The growing diversity of school demographics indicate there will be more and more people with migrant backgrounds subscribing to an independent education. These cohorts will want to be valued and connected. Schools should therefore make certain their attitudes, the language used and the people they recruit to serve as volunteers are drawn from a cross-section of its community.

The future of philanthropy is already here. It involves connecting with more people to secure donations. The size of the gift is less important compared to the number of donors. The social media ecosystem can easily and effectively promote stories of gifts and how they have helped students. Donors are now focusing on making sure their donation will make an impact. They will seek assurances that their gift will result in improving the lives of others. They want to know how an assessment of the initiative will be achieved so there is verity attached to the results.

So how does this relate to the school context? Figure 2 below summarises the growth of a donor's development. Schools can play a part in this development by being a partner at any of these stages. At first it is about making a donation. Then the donor considers organising their giving and develops a budget. Confidence and knowledge are gained, and they learn about a particular project the school wants to initiate. Once inspired, the donor can activate and leverage their networks to gain a maximum benefit for the school and their commitment.

Figure 2: Growth of a Donor's Development

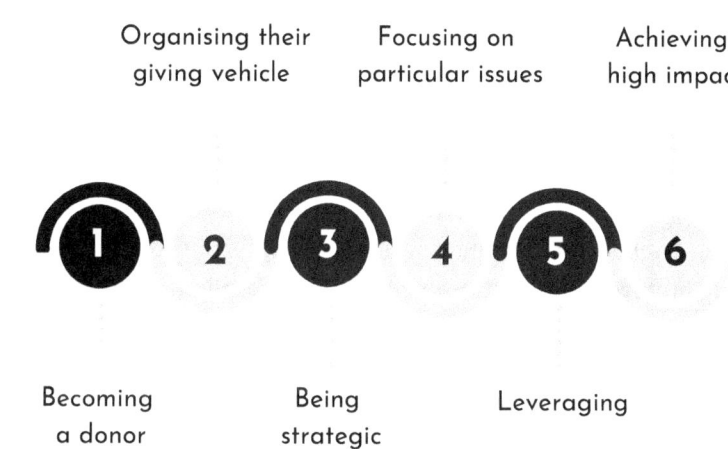

Another change worth noting is that contemporary philanthropy is shifting away from anonymous giving. Donors are now more willing to add their name to a list and champion the reasons that motivated them to give, thus providing an example for others to follow. Furthermore, there are several instances of leading business people pledging to give away large portions of their accumulated wealth during their lifetime. Warren Buffet and Bill Gates come to mind, and in Australia we can add to the list include Nicola and Andrew Forrest, Craig and Di Winkler and Paul Bassat.

Some people simply make donations from their own bank account, whilst others prefer to establish a foundation, usually a private ancillary fund (PAF). Melburnian couple Craig and Di Winkler established the Yajilarra Trust with a gift of more than $100 million. Andrew and Nicola Forrest set up the Minderoo Foundation, which now has a corpus of $1.5 billion.

Paul Ramsay left his entire estate, about $3.6 billion, to establish the Paul Ramsay Foundation. Brian Davis made a bequest to boost his foundation so that it now has a corpus of well in excess of $100 million. These sums may seem out of reach for schools—and this is probably true—but the points to take home are that large gifts are possible and endowments are potent. Simply make friends first and have a vision.

The wealthy people mentioned above are challenging the tall poppy syndrome. Their overt advocacy for giving and philanthropy has provided the direction necessary to shift perceptions about wealthy people. They are wanting to contribute to a better society and a better world, and their actions speak louder than words. This shift in people's view of giving will incentivise more people to become donors. A school's key stakeholders will be hearing these conversations. The penny will drop.

Schools should share their stories about the role of benevolence in their evolution. Each school will have its stories. This is part of establishing an enduring culture of philanthropy. A culture of philanthropy is inclusive and aims to connect with people and engage in a school's evolution. It is more about supporting a vision than a need.

A proposed first step to create a culture of giving and inspire prospective donors is to consider establishing named honours, such as:

- prizes recognising academic excellence or progress
- awards recognising non-academic achievements, such as sport or school service
- scholarships offering fee relief for academic excellence or progress
- bursaries offering fee relief for those experiencing financial hardship or to boost diversity in the student body
- teaching fellowships providing financial support to underwrite teacher professional development
- an innovators fund supporting student initiatives
- a memorial fund honouring a lost loved one with a gift that can be invested in perpetuity and used at the principal's discretion or used to purchase and plant a memorial tree, for example.

As shown in Table 7 below, the sums needed to endow these honours varies. Naturally scholarships and bursaries require greater sums, and these will depend on the level of tuition fees. It is recommended that a school starts by seeking funds to endow prizes and awards because the sum needed is more modest. These endowed honours would be listed in the annual school presentation night program. The audience will have plenty of time to read through the program and discover the number—or perhaps the lack—of named honours, which will inevitably plant a seed. Reading the family names in the program gives depth and a sense of longevity to benevolence at your school. Of course, a list can also be presented in the philanthropy section of a school's website.

Table 7: Recommended Sums to Endow Different Honours

Honour	Perpetual Endowment Sum	Annual Return (5%)	Distribution	Admin to School	Return to Corpus
Prize	$5,000	$250	$125	$20	$105
Award	$5,000	$250	$125	$20	$105
Teaching fellowship	$50,000	2,500	$2,250	$50	$200
Innovators fund	$10,000		$10,000		
Scholarship (full)*	$400,000	$20,000	$19,000	$50	$950
Scholarship (half)*	$200,000	$10,000	$9,000	$50	$950
Bursary (full)*	$400,000	$20,000	$19,000	$50	$950
Bursary (half)*	$200,000	$10,000	$9,000	$50	$950

*Based on Year 12 tuition fees of $20,000 per annum

People can feel they are not important enough to have their name connected to an honour, thinking this option is only available to a school's hierarchy or inner sanctum. Seeking one or two gifts from those outside the immediate school family will start to dispel this misconception. As the stories of new donors are shared, others will be motivated to follow suit. The stories attached to the establishment of an endowed honour will help promote further endowments and the notion of giving as a proud tradition. Such stories will also add a different dimension to the history of a school and are an important part of its maturity.

Schools are places of learning that vibrate with the enthusiasm of youth. They offer myriad opportunities and countless combinations of people with enthusiasm and optimism. Philanthropy, the love of humankind, has a valid place in every school.

APPENDICES

Appendix 1	Key Elements of a Culture of Philanthropy in a School
Appendix 2	Philanthropy Working Party Terms of Reference
Appendix 3	Philanthropy Working Party Meeting Guidelines
Appendix 4	Memorandum of Gift Template
Appendix 5	Memorandum of Understanding Template
Appendix 6	Functions Checklist
Appendix 7	Gift Submission Example: Student Leadership Program
Appendix 8	Donation/Pledge Form Template
Appendix 9	Receipt Letter Example
Appendix 10	Bequest Form Template
Appendix 11	Codicil Template
Appendix 12	Thanking Guidelines
Appendix 13	Donor Commitment Continuum
Appendix 14	Useful Words and Phrases

APPENDIX I

KEY ELEMENTS OF A CULTURE OF PHILANTHROPY IN A SCHOOL

Those connected to the school should see themselves as ambassadors. They should build relationships and speak with pride about the vision and successes of the school. The voice is a critical element of philanthropy. Prospective donors will respond when the school's leaders promote the vision and show loyalty, pride and passion.

School leaders can carefully and strategically create and manage the appropriate strategies and atmosphere that will form the basis of an enduring culture of philanthropy by:

- creating a compelling vision
- forming a unified committee (working party) that brings key constituents together so they can learn from and support one another
- establishing a supportive legal framework and operational and governance guidelines for volunteer working parties (committees)
- practising stewardship (maintaining relationships) and thanking those who have supported the school as donors, friends, volunteers and advocates
- hosting functions, reunions, VIP events, anniversaries and events with the local community
- ensuring philanthropy is a regular item on the board agenda
- encouraging board members, staff, parents and students to be committed ambassadors of the school
- involving board members and senior executives in securing donations
- establishing database management guidelines and procedures
- promoting database management as a skilled and respected function

- ensuring donors and donations are not a hidden topic
- committing to the process, ensuring it is adequately resourced, with agreed time frames and milestones
- providing documents to guide how meetings operate, including an adult code of conduct and terms of reference for working parties that define their purpose and remit
- publishing information about philanthropy on the school's website and in the yearbook
- providing active guidelines for thanking and receipting (e.g. receipts are issued within three business days)
- sharing information about philanthropy during the new staff and board member recruitment process
- including stories about philanthropy in the prospective parent information pack.

APPENDIX 2

PHILANTHROPY WORKING PARTY TERMS OF REFERENCE

Establishment

The ABC College Philanthropy Working Party (PWP) is a group composed of staff and volunteers established by the Board and supported by the Principal to empower the growth of an enduring culture of philanthropy at the College. It is not a legal entity and has no constitution because this avoids the need for auditing costs, legal obligations and regulations determined by the Australian Charities and Not-for-profits Commission. The PWP records actions, plans, recommendations and decisions as Meeting Notes rather than Minutes.

Philanthropy is defined as 'the love of humankind', and so the preferred focus of this group is to connect with and engage people.

Role and Purpose

- To establish an enduring culture of philanthropy within the College's community.
- To establish and maintain meaningful relations with donors, parents, staff, students, alumni, volunteers, neighbours and local key stakeholders.
- To craft a compelling philanthropic vision that is broadcast to the community.
- To provide the leadership and overview of initiatives associated with raising funds for the College and its programs, including project funding, endowments, fundraising events, sponsorships, appeals, bequests, thanking and stewardship.
- To be a relevant and astute entity that provides advice and strategies to the College about philanthropy and community engagement and is empowered to do same.

- To recruit members with diverse skills who believe in the philanthropic vision of the College.
- To ensure the College runs its database effectively and knows how to check its governance and statutory requirements.

Membership

The PWP will consist of representatives of the College's key constituents who are appointed by the Chair, proportionally allocated to reflect a diversity of representation. For example, donors, staff, past staff, alumni, Board members, local community leaders and volunteers.

- The PWP will consist of a minimum of 11 persons and a maximum of 19.
- A Board member will chair this group. The Principal is ex officio.
- Additional resources can be co-opted by the PWP to address skills or knowledge shortages or to assist with special projects.

Structure

The PWP operates with a flat structure that prompts an open and transparent exchange of thoughts and ideas. Three subgroups are formed to ensure there is a focus on the necessary actions so the group can deliver outcomes. The three groups are:

- Finance, Resources and Investments
- Communications, Strategy and Planning
- Donor and Community Engagement.

Subgroups other than those listed above may be added at the discretion of the group. Members are to align themselves to the subgroup they feel most connected to and where they see their skills and experience are a natural fit.

A set of Meeting Guidelines that describe the expectations of members accompanies these Terms of Reference.

APPENDIX 3

PHILANTHROPY WORKING PARTY PWP MEETING GUIDELINES

These guidelines are to assist current and future members of the ABC College Philanthropy Working Party (PWP) to appreciate the expectations, roles and responsibilities associated with joining this group. They reflect the mutual regard between members and the overall objectives of the PWP.

1. The PWP welcomes a blend of individuals who represent the different constituents of the College.
2. The PWP agrees to understand and adopt best practices.
3. PWP members are expected to read and consider the contents of Meeting Notes, briefing papers and reference documents in a timely manner.
4. PWP members are expected to contribute to the overall objectives of the group in a collegiate manner and conduct themselves in an open-minded fashion.
5. PWP members are required to uphold the College's values.
6. Working Party meetings are held in the evenings on a set day of the week and are scheduled to last no more than 90 minutes. It is expected that members will attend all meetings except where an absence is unavoidable and for pre-advised reasons.
7. PWP members will act in the best interests of the group and the College and advocate a consistent and professional message about the purpose of the organisation.
8. From time to time, and as required to perform relevant tasks, members may be privy to information that is sensitive. Such information must be kept confidential and be used only for the purpose for which it is intended.

9. Members must ensure that all financial and governance matters, including those relating to fundraising and donations, are managed transparently, responsibly and with appropriate reference to the organisation's policies and procedures.
10. The Board is to be kept informed of all matters by the PWP.
11. A member can resign at any time. Where possible, reasonable notice should be provided. Members retiring are encouraged to recommend their replacement.
12. The PWP Chair may from time to time rotate members among various subgroups.
13. PWP Chair or the Board may discontinue the tenure of members where it is deemed that a change of membership is in the best interest of the group's purpose.
14. Subject to the Chair's discretion, a person's inclusion may lapse if his/her absence is recorded in four consecutive meetings.
15. The PWP will be chaired by a Board member, and members will select a secretary.

APPENDIX 4

MEMORANDUM OF GIFT TEMPLATE

The donor(s) intends to make the gift to ABC College (ABC) (ABN 123456789), upon the terms set out in this memorandum.

1. _____
                              (name/s)

   of _____
                              (address)

2. **Gift**

The donor will donate the sum of $ _____ to a nominated fund administered and owned by _____, whose ABN is _____, upon the terms set out in this memorandum.

Any obligations of ABC are conditional on all such amounts being received. If all amounts are not received, ABC reserves the right to apply monies received for a purpose that is as close as possible to the stated purpose.

The nominated fund represented by the gift is able to receive additional donations or bequests for the stated purpose or the alternate purpose and may be supplemented from ABC funds or any other legitimate source.

3. **Stated purpose**

The gift is to establish an award/prize/fellowship to be granted annually, to recognise excellence in _____ OR progress in _____.

The sum donated will generate an annual return. The annual return is the maximum sum that can support this award/prize/fellowship. Some earnings will be reinvested into the corpus each year. ABC's Investment Policy determines how funds are invested. An annual return of 5% is assumed.

4. **Establishment of an Endowment**

When the donor makes the gift, a separate ledger within the ABC Endowment Fund will be created for the stated purpose and ABC will be the trustee and manager of the fund.

5. **Period of benefit from the gift**

Subject to clause 2 (Gift), the donor makes the gift to establish a perpetual endowment for the stated purpose, meaning that in perpetuity ABC in its capacity as trustee will invest with a view to enhancing over time the capital sum represented by the gift and will apply the income arising from the gift for the stated purpose.

6. **Timing of first award**

An award can usually only be made after the preceding year's net annual income has been quantified and then only if that income is sufficient to finance the award.

The award is to be first awarded in YYYY, and the value of the award on that occasion is to be the net income from the date of the signed document to three months before the award is given.

7. **Treatment of Unspent Income**

Any unexpended income in any year may be:

- retained as income, in which case it will be available in any subsequent year to be applied for the stated purpose; *and/or*
- added to the capital sum established by the gift, in which case that unexpended income will be forever regarded as capital and will therefore be preserved.

8. Proposed name of award

The proposed name for the award endowed by the gift is
'_____,'
The donor requests that this name be used when describing each award.

9. Reporting back to the donor

The donor will receive a receipt from ABC corresponding with each donation.

The donor will receive an annual report from ABC detailing financial performance of the endowment and expenditure details.

10. Donor recognition

The donor may wish to be anonymous. If the donor agrees that he/she is willing to be referenced in publicity and promotional material, including donor honour rolls relating to the gift, the name used will be

_____

ABC will gain the donor's approval for any promotional material or publicity relating to the gift that mentions the donor's name prior to it being produced or released.

11. Public disclosure

ABC may disclose publicly the value of the gift and the stated purpose. These details are typically published by ABC in a summary or annual report that are accessible to the public as a subset of knowledge in the annual report to the Australian Charities and Not-for-profits Commission.

The donor(s) directs ABC to describe the gift publicly as a gift from the donor(s). Accordingly, with respect to the gift, the donor(s) authorises ABC to disclose publicly the following personal information regarding the donor (as that information is recorded in this memorandum): the donor's name and association with ABC.

Where applicable, the donor also authorises ABC to disclose publicly the donor's relationship to any recipient of the award. See also the Privacy Statement that forms part of this memorandum.

12. Recording the terms of the gift

This memorandum records all the terms of the gift and supersedes any earlier communications between the donor and ABC regarding the terms of the gift.

13. ABC trust record and administrative arrangements

ABC's obligations as trustee will be reflected in an account record that may also contain administrative arrangements made and amended by ABC from time to time in order to implement and perform the stated purpose.

14. Terms of the gift cannot be altered later

The donor acknowledges that the donor cannot alter the terms upon which the gift is made after making the gift (or any part of the gift) to ABC.

15. Legal advice to the donor

The donor has had an opportunity to obtain independent legal advice regarding the gift and any taxation consequences, and this memorandum.

16. Privacy Statement

Privacy legislation: ABC has a statutory obligation to comply with the *Privacy and Data Protection Act 2014* (Victoria) in its treatment of personal information.

Purposes of collection of personal information: ABC collects personal information about a donor, principally for the purposes of receiving, receipting, recording and administering a gift.

Disclosure of personal information: ABC will not disclose publicly a donor's personal information unless the donor has given consent for that disclosure to occur or unless ABC is permitted or required by law to do so. Accuracy, security and storage of personal information: ABC holds personal information in the form of electronic and paper-based records. It takes all reasonable steps to ensure that the personal information it holds is accurate, complete and protected from misuse, loss, unauthorised access or disclosure.

Access to personal information: A donor may access his or her personal information held by ABC. Access to and correction of a donor's personal information is governed by the *Privacy and Data Protection Act 2014* (Victoria).

Privacy Officer: ABC's chief Privacy Officer is the Principal.

Donor name(s) _____

_____   ___ / ___ / _____
              signature   dd   mm   yyyy

on behalf of ABC

_____   _____
           name   title

Signature   _____

Witnessed by   _____
                                name

Signature   _____

APPENDIX 5

MEMORANDUM OF UNDERSTANDING TEMPLATE

This Memorandum of Understanding (MOU) is between ABC College (ABC) (ABN 123456789) and _____ (ABN 1234567890), the Visitor.

This MOU outlines the provision of advice, services, equipment, and Intellectual Property (IP) for ABC in regard to

_____

Expectations

It is expected that parties will operate at the highest professional standard and provide information and services described herein that are current, plausible and regarded as best practice.

It is expected that ABC and _____ will be as responsive as possible.

Fee

There is no fee.

Or

The monthly fee payable is $_____ plus GST, payable on a set day each month from XX month to XX month YYYY. The fee is all inclusive and no other charges can be levied.

Contact

Contacts between the nominated persons representing each partner in this MOU are by mutual agreement but should be a minimum of ____ times a month. Regular communication can be via phone, zoom or email between scheduled meetings.

Topics outlined below determine the priorities of this MOU but are not exclusive and may change as knowledge and information comes to light and people and priorities change.

Purpose

Advice	relating to plans, strategies and actions congruent with and supportive of community engagement, database management, staff and executive training, and philanthropy and financial investment options
Counsel	relating to the implementation of any of the projects or advice
Training	the MOU includes the training by the Visitor for staff at all levels of ABC in respect to topics described in this MOU
Documents	the Visitor provides documents and reference material as part of the engagement. ABC provides appropriate storage facilities for such documents, either in hard or soft copy.

_____   _____

Allan Smith   Jill Brown
CEO   The Visitor
ABC College

/   /   /   /
dd   mm   yyyy   dd   mm   yyyy

_____   _____

name of witness   signature of witness

APPENDIX 6

FUNCTIONS CHECKLIST

People remember how they were made to feel at an event more than what was said.

Stage	Items
Preparation	- Define the purpose of the event: inspire, thank, connect. - Check diaries of dignitaries, school calendar, facility availability, public holidays, access and security etc. - Decide who to invite and how invites will be issued (post, email, letter, phone call). - Determine whether the event will be cost neutral or subsidised by the school. - Get quotes from caterer and match food to the audience. - Explain current COVID-19 requirements.
Type of Event	- Decide the type of event: breakfast, morning tea, lunch, afternoon tea, drinks or dinner. - Match the event to the purpose, the importance and age of those to be invited. Morning tea or lunch is more suited to an older audience (e.g. bequestors and past staff); dinner with the principal is more engaging for current parents.

Stage	Items
Event Preparation	• Set up meet-and-greet table, name tags, tables, chairs, banners etc. • Organise direction signage, banners, lighting (check internal and external lighting beforehand) heating/cooling, AV etc. • Know how to lock and unlock rooms. • Have a first-aid kit on hand and arrange for a member of staff with a current first-aid certificate attend the event. • Organise car parking and security. • Plan catering to suit the audience, budget and season. • Seek info about dietary requirements and avoid unfamiliar foods.
Key Message(s)	• Ensure key message(s) is matched to the purpose of the event, as indicated in the invitation. Ensure people are given messages clearly with little waffle. • Decide who will deliver the message and who will thank people for their participation.
Equipment	• Check tables, chairs etc are appropriate. • Check overhead projectors, computer connections, furniture, rest rooms, access etc. • Prepare slide show, banners, decorations, gifts etc.
Briefing	• Brief speakers about their role and emphasise they need to follow the running sheet • Brief key personnel about the number of guests attending and the VIPs to engage with during the function • Prepare speech notes: Thank you for coming. Why are we here? The purpose of tonight/today is to … key points etc. • Events should have a beginning, a middle and an end.

Stage	Items

Running Sheet and Timing	• Send a running sheet with timing of each item detailed in minutes to the key people (caterer, host, speakers etc) 24 hours before the event.
	• Organise meet-and-greet table people (host, staff, volunteers).
	• Organise who will give:
	  • welcome address
	  • 'thank you for coming' speech
	  • toast to the school.
	• Start and finish on time.

Follow-up	• Send thank-you notes within four weeks. • If appropriate to the occasion, report on progress/outcomes about four months after the event.
Debrief and Database	• Record those invited and their RSVPs in the database. • Debrief with staff and volunteers. • Add anecdotes about attendees to database.

APPENDIX 7

GIFT SUBMISSION EXAMPLE: STUDENT LEADERSHIP PROGRAM

Date	1 April 2022
Context	The permanent endowment of a student leadership program. An annual program to assist the College's Year 12 students to be engaged, skilled leaders of the school. The endowment would help pay for the training program in January before the start of Term 1 each year.
Gift	$30,000
Recognition	The gift can be anonymous, or a name can be given to the program.
Purpose	Provide funds (50%) so the College can engage specialist experts in youth leadership so the new Year 12 leaders are well-trained and capable leaders.
Benefits	*Students*: Student leaders feel confident to be effective leaders of their peers.
	Staff: Staff feel proud that the College is investing in students.
	College: The College's reputation for empowering students is enhanced.
	Parents: Parents are pleased to learn students are taught valuable skills that will be useful in future years.

Expected Outcomes	The student leaders will be skilled in leadership and better able to fulfil their duties. Senior staff will be better equipped and know more about contemporary communications, such as social media.
College Contribution	$2,000 per annum (total cost each year $3,500, $2,000 from school and $1,500 from investment income)
Time Frame	The start of 2023
Project	External experts will attend the College for two days to inform, train and inspire the College student leaders. The program will cover: • public speaking/body language • communicating with peers • how to respond to questions and how to use a microphone • use of speech notes • how to thank/acknowledge people according to their status and relation with the College
Detail	An intensive two-day learning experience for student leaders before Term 1 begins. Students will learn from modern communications experts, psychologists and principals from other schools about how best to present to their peers and engage with the general student body in Years 7–12. They will also be given details about effective time management, speaking skills and deportment.

APPENDIX 8

DONATION/PLEDGE FORM TEMPLATE

Insert above school livery, badge etc

Insert below phrases of your choice, for example:

We believe our school is a daring adventure where children learn to think for themselves, in preparation for a future of exciting possibilities.

DONATION/PLEDGE FORM

I/We want to support ABC College and its students with a pledge.

Annual sum $ _____ over _____ years

or

Single gift $ _____

Please acknowledge this gift as:

☐ Anonymous

☐ Parents _____
                 name(s)

☐ Grandparents _____
                 name(s)

☐ Alumni Year ____ _____
                 name(s)

☐ Past staff _____
                 name(s)

☐ Friend _____
                 name(s)

☐ Please find enclosed a cheque

or

☐ Please debit this credit card VISA / MC*

_ _ _ _   _ _ _ _   _ _ _ _   _ _ _ _

Expiry __ / __

Name on card _____

* once processed these details will be destroyed

I/We would like this gift to be directed to:

☐ The Building Fund
☐ The Scholarship Fund

Gifts to these funds are tax deductible

Thank You

APPENDIX 9

RECEIPT LETTER EXAMPLE

On school letterhead

1 February 2023

Ms A Browning
1 Smith Street
SMITHSVILLE VIC 3007

Dear Ms Browning

Thank you for your donation in support of the College. Each year I am pleased to thank over 100 families who support the College with a voluntary contribution. Like you, I am also a donor.

Donations to the Building Fund assist us to refurbish and improve College facilities. The most recent donations have contributed to the construction of a media room for the Middle Years, upgrades to the Years 5 & 6 area and further development of the Senior School virtual library.

This year, donations will be directed to support improvements to the College's Years 7 & 8 area.

Once a year we host a thank-you function for our donors, so please consider joining this year's thank-you breakfast at 7.30 am on 8 October. I look forward to meeting and thanking you personally at this event.

Please find your receipt details below.

Yours sincerely

Simon Smith
Principal

Date	1 June 2022
Name	Ms A Browning
Fund	Building Fund
Donation	$200
Receipt No.	2015001

Donations over $2 are tax deductible.

APPENDIX 10

BEQUEST FORM TEMPLATE

I,_____
                                    (name/s)

of _____
                                    (address)

give, free of all duties and taxes to ABC College, 16 Main Road, SMITHSVILLE VIC 3840 (ABN 123456789) for its general purposes the following:

- The whole or _____ % of the residue of my estate
- The whole or _____ % of my estate
- The sum of $ _____
- OR _____
  (details of a particular asset—such as shares, art works, collectibles or property)

☐ It is my wish that this gift be used at the Principal's discretion
☐ It is my wish that this gift be used at the Principal's discretion and request it be used to support _____
☐ It is my wish that this gift be invested in perpetuity in the College's Endowment Fund and the interest earned used to support:
  ☐ A student bursary
  ☐ A student scholarship
  ☐ The staff professional development program
  ☐ A prize or award
  ☐ Other _____

A receipt from ABC College's authorised officer will be a sufficient discharge for the executor(s) or trustee(s) of my estate.

_____   /   /
           signature   dd mm yyyy

Witnessed by the following persons who have signed their names in the presence of each other and of the person named above.

_____	_____
name of witness	name of witness
_____	_____
occupation	occupation
_____	_____
address	address
_____	_____
signature	signature

APPENDIX II

CODICIL TEMPLATE

I, _____
                         (name/s)

of _____
                         (address)

Declare this to be a Codicil of my Will that is dated ....

I give to ABC College (ABN 123456789):

- the whole (or _____ %) of the residue of my estate
- the whole (or _____ %) of my estate
- the sum of $ _____

The ticked box(es) below indicate(s) my preference(s).
☐ It is my wish that this gift be used at the Principal's discretion.
☐ It is my wish that this gift be used at the Principal's discretion and request it be used to support _____
☐ It is my wish that this gift be invested in perpetuity in the College's Endowment Fund and the interest earned directed to support:
    ☐ A student bursary
    ☐ A student scholarship
    ☐ The staff professional development program
    ☐ The Student Amenity Fund
    ☐ The Library Fund
    ☐ The Building Fund

In all other respects I confirm my Will.

Signed by the testator in our presence and attested by us both of the testator and of each other.

_____   /   /
               signature   dd   mm   yyyy

Witnessed by the following persons who have signed their names in the presence of each other and of the person named above.

_____   _____
name of witness   name of witness

_____   _____
occupation   occupation

_____   _____
address   address

_____   _____
signature   signature

APPENDIX 12

THANKING GUIDELINES

This document provides guidelines for how ABC College thanks its donors. Every donation of money/gift/time is important and should be thanked and acknowledged.

Establishing a framework and good habits ensures we:

- thank in an appropriate manner that reflects the gift/time/donation
- avoid over-thanking when multiple stakeholders thank for the same gift
- do not under-thank
- are consistent with our thanking
- record all donations (time/gift/money) in Synergetic.

An example of inconsistent thanking: one donor gives $1,000 and receives a computer-generated receipt without personalisation, while another donor gives $30 worth of chocolates and gets a thank-you note, a phone call and a mention in the College's weekly email to parents.

The following should be applied when thanking donors to the College.

Voluntary Contribution Made with Fee Payments		
Acknowledgement		
Synergetic-generated receipt and letter from Principal	✓	
Included on donor lists (website and honour board)	✓	
Invited to annual donor/volunteer thank-you event	✓	
Thank-you call from PWP Chair or Principal	✓	20 donations

Donations other than Voluntary Contributions				
Acknowledgement	**Donation Range**			
	$2 – $99	$100 – $999	$1,000 – $4,999	$5,000+
Computer-generated receipt and letter from Principal	✓	✓	✓	✓
Personalised handwritten note with receipt from PWP Chair			✓	✓
Personal phone call from Principal				✓
Included on donor lists (website and honour board)	✓	✓	✓	✓
Invite to thank-you event	✓	✓	✓	✓

Gifts in Kind				
Acknowledgement	**Estimated Gift Value**			
	$2 – $99	$100 – $499	$500 – $499	$1,000+
Thank-you email/letter from event/program organiser	✓	✓		
Thank-you letter/email from PWP Chair			✓	✓
Thank-you call from Principal/ PWP Chair/Head of School			✓	✓
Included on donor lists (website and honour board)	✓	✓	✓	✓
Invite to annual volunteer/donor thank-you event	✓	✓	✓	✓

APPENDIX 13

DONOR COMMITMENT CONTINUUM*

Attributes / Description	Ignorance	Awareness	Interest	Experience	Participation	Ownership
	Does not know why the organisation needs money	Has heard of the building fund and the scholarship fund	Shares the organisation's values	Has seen/heard/felt the results of the organisation	Volunteers for the benefit of the organisation	Volunteers to serve on committees
	Does not know about previous donors and their stories	Is aware of names of donors around the organisation	Believes the organisation warrants support	Knows people in the organisation	Feels part of the organisation	Considers the organisation is a part of my mission in life
			Is likely to read or scan the organisation's collateral	Attends organisation events	Trusts the people in the organisation's leadership positions	Seeks ways to advance the organisation's reputation and good work
			Will speak well of the organisation (be an advocate) and can tell stories	Believes in the organisation's leadership	Is an active advocate for the organisation	Invests a large portion of their philanthropy in the organisation
				Is a donor to the organisation	Would like to make larger gifts	Proud of their involvement with the organisation

*Adapted for Australian use by Gavan Woinarski from a document produced by Advancement Resources (USA), founded by Joe Golding.

APPENDIX 14

USEFUL WORDS AND PHRASES

Philanthropy is derived from the Greek words *philos* (loving/friend) and *anthropos* (humankind).

Philanthropy literally means 'the love of humankind'. It involves the giving of time, resources, talent or money for the benefit of other people. It focuses on the elimination of social problems, diseases and hardships or on pioneering new ideas.

Philanthropy's greatest partner is your voice.

Philanthropy responds to a vision more than a need.

Philanthropy is the transfer of private assets for public good.

References to philanthropy can be found in the Qur'an, Bible and Torah and in the teachings of other religions and sects in India, Japan, China and North America. There is evidence of philanthropy dating back 4,000 years.

Philanthropy and fundraising are not synonyms. Fundraising is tactical, whereas philanthropy is relational.

Consider the language used around philanthropy, for example:

- wealth, work and wisdom
- time, talent and treasure
- give, get, or get off
- 'prospects', not 'targets'
- 'connect and inspire', not 'hit them up'.

Starting and Steering the Conversation

Asking is personal, so it should be done face to face. Some gentle ways to start and steer the conversation are:

- 'Would you and your family feel comfortable giving /would you please consider a gift of $_____ for the _____ project?'
- 'I am a donor, and I would like to ask you to join with me by making a gift you are proud of. We are hoping your family might consider a gift of $_____'
- 'I am making calls ahead of our June parents and friends meeting to touch base with each member of the group. How are things for you? Have you had a good week?'
- 'Would you have a few moments to catch-up, please?'
- 'Thank you for listening and taking an interest. Would you please consider a gift at some stage? We could reconnect and discuss this in a few weeks.'
- 'Can we share the story of you gift with others?'

Limerick

The event was planned and invites sent
Costs were low; they spent less than a cent.
The big day arrived but nobody came,
It was hard to find a reason to name.
'We forgot to say thanks. Is this what they meant?'

Everyone wanted the gifts to roll in,
They went to the post box and put the letters in.
They waited and waited and felt alone,
Then someone said, 'Pick up the phone.'
The donors reacted and created a win-win.

GLOSSARY

ACNC	Australian Charities and Not-for-profits Commission
Award	A non-academic honour given to a student for a particular purpose
Bequest	A gift in a will to a person or entity
Bursary	Fee relief given to a student's family because of financial hardship
Codicil	A single-page document attached to a will giving additional instructions
Corpus	A sum of money that is invested and never spent
CRM database	Customer relationship management database
DGR	Deductible Gift Recipient: the official description of an organisation that can accept tax-deductible donations

Endowment fund	A fund owned and administered by an organisation that is separate from the organisation's main accounts (the fund holds an amount—the corpus—which is never spent, and only the income generated from the fund's investments can be spent)
ESG	The financial industry acronym that describes ethical investments (environment, social and governance)
Ethical	The notion that investments should be made in entities that do not benefit from slave labour, the promotion of gambling, the sale of tobacco, natural habitat exploitation, wage theft etc
Fellowship	A sum of money allocated for the professional development of a teacher
Franking credit	The franked amount of a dividend that can be claimed back from the Australian Tax Office by a not-for-profit
Honours	Collective noun to describe prizes, awards, fellowships etc
PAF	Private Ancillary Fund: a fund established by an individual from which distributions are made to DGRs
Perpetuity	No finite end
Philanthropy	The love of humankind
Prize	An honour given to a student for academic excellence or in recognition of academic progress
PuAF	Public Ancillary Fund: a fund that can accept donations from different sources and make distributions to DGRs
PWP	Philanthropy Working Party

Scholarship	A reduction in the tuition fee in recognition of academic potential, progress or excellence
Stewardship	The thoughtful and strategic ongoing management of relations with key constituents
Thanking	Personalised recognition and acknowledgement

BIBLIOGRAPHY

Ashman A and Elkins J (2008) *Education for Inclusion and Diversity*, 3rd edn, Pearson Education Australia, Canada.

Brown CJ (2010) *Great Foundations*, ACER Press, Melbourne.

Buchanan P (2019) *Giving Done Right*, PublicAffairs, New York.

Cheng M (2019) '8 Characteristics of Millennials That Support Sustainable Development Goals', *Forbes*, accessed 5 December 2022. https://www.forbes.com/sites/margueritacheng/2019/06/19/8-characteristics-of-millennials-that-support-sustainable-development-goals-sdgs/?sh=31cf809429b7

Deloitte (n.d.) 'What's Next for Philanthropy in the 2020s?', Deloitte website, accessed 5 December 2022. https://www2.deloitte.com/us/en/pages/about-deloitte/articles/preparing-for-the-future-of-philanthropy.html

Drucker P (2001) *The Essential Drucker*, Harper Business, New York.

Epstein MJ and Warren McFarlan F (2011) *Joining a Nonprofit Board: What You Need to Know*, Jossey-Bass, San Francisco.

Equity Trustees (n.d.) 'The Alfred Felton Bequest', Equity Trustees website, accessed 5 December 2022. https://www.eqt.com.au/philanthropy/the-alfred-felton-bequest

Fidelity Charitable (2021) 'The Future of Philanthropy', Fidelity Charitable website, accessed 5 December 2022. https://www.fidelitycharitable.org/content/dam/fc-public/docs/resources/2021-future-of-philanthropy-summary.pdf

Garcia A (2016) 'Nike's Phil Knight gives $400 million to Stanford University', *CNN Money*, accessed 5 December 2022. https://money.cnn.com/2016/02/24/news/nike-phil-knight-stanford-donation/index.html

Gibson CM (n.d.) 'Beyond Fundraising. What Does it Mean to Build a Culture of Philanthropy?', Evelyn and Walter Haas, Jr. Fund, accessed 5 December 2022. https://www.haasjr.org/sites/default/files/resources/Haas_CultureofPhilanthropy_F1_0.pdf

Kentucky Department of Education (2022) 'School District Personnel Information: Average Certified Salaries', Kentucky Department of Education website, accessed 5 December 2022. https://education.ky.gov/districts/FinRept/Pages/School%20District%20Personnel%20Information.aspx

KPMG (n.d.) 'The Future of Philanthropy', KPMG website, accessed 5 December 2022. https://home.kpmg/xx/en/home/insights/2021/08/the-future-of-philanthropy.html

Nietzel MT (2022) 'Phil and Penny Knight Give $75 Million to Stanford University to Study Brain Resilience', *Forbes*, accessed 5 December 2022. https://www.forbes.com/sites/michaeltnietzel/2022/04/27/phil-and-penny-knight-give-75-million-to-stanford-university-to-study-brain-resilience/?sh=72ba07ce3a52

Only Melbourne (n.d.) 'Macpherson Robertson (Sir)', Only Melbourne website, accessed 5 December 2022. https://www.onlymelbourne.com.au/macpherson-robertson-sir

Philanthropy Squared (2015) 'Joe Golding, CEO Advancement Resources (USA)', Philanthropy Squared website, accessed 5 December 2022. https://philanthropy2.com/thinkery/lorem-ipsum-dolor-sit-amet-consectetur

Radbourne J and Watkins K (2015) *Philanthropy and the Arts*, Melbourne University Publishing, Melbourne.

Sinek S (2014) 'How Great Leaders Inspire Action' [video], TED website, accessed 5 December 2022. https://www.ted.com/talks/simon_sinek_how_great_leaders_inspire_action?language=en

Stanford University (n.d) 'A History of Stanford', Stanford University website, accessed 5 December 2022. https://www.stanford.edu/about/history/

Wyatt Trust (n.d) 'About Us', The Wyatt Benevolent Institution website, accessed 5 December 2022. https://wyatt.org.au/about-us/

Yale University (n.d.) 'Traditions and History', Yale University website, accessed 5 December 2022. https://www.yale.edu/about-yale/traditions-history

www.ingramcontent.com/pod-product-compliance
Lightning Source LLC
Chambersburg PA
CBHW050029130526
44590CB00042B/2355